Fresh Herbs

FRESH HERBS

Over 100 Uses for Growing, Cooking, Cosmetics, and Garden Design

BARBARA RADCLIFFE ROGERS

GALLERY BOOKS

An Imprint of W.H. Smith Publishers, Inc.
112 Madison Avenue
New York, New York 10016

Dedication

In loving memory of Pat Greene, whose garden always delighted and inspired me, and whose love of growing things lives on through all of us who knew her.

A FRIEDMAN GROUP BOOK

Published by GALLERY BOOKS
An imprint of W.H. Smith Publishers, Inc.
112 Madison Avenue
New York, New York 10016

ISBN 0-8317-3574-0

FRESH HERBS: Over 100 Uses for Growing, Cooking, Cosmetics, and Garden Design
was prepared and produced by
Michael Friedman Publishing Group, Inc.
15 West 26th Street
New York, NY 10010

Editor: Sharon Kalman
Designer: Susan Hood
Photography Editor: Christopher Bain
Production Manager: Karen L. Greenberg

Typeset by BPE Graphics
Color separations by United South Sea Graphic Art Co., Ltd.
Printed and bound in Hong Kong by Leefung-Asco Printers Ltd.

Gallery Books are available for bulk purchase and premium use. For details write or telephone the Manager of Special Sales, W.H. Smith Publishers, Inc., 112 Madison Avenue, New York, New York 10016 (212) 532-6600

This book is intended as a reference only. The use of fresh herbs in cooking or as a cosmetic should not be attempted by those suffering from allergies without the advice of a physician. The information presented here is not to substitute for any treatment prescribed by a physician.

Additional Photo Credits
© Steven Mark Needham/ Envision, pg. 3
© Michael Grand, pg. 9, 43

In Appreciation

Herb growers must be among the world's friendliest and most generous people. All you need do is mention a project or an interest and help comes from all directions.

So it was with this book. As I look through the manuscript, it is like a memory album of old friends, new friends, and friends by mail. Some of the ideas have traveled so far and through so many people that I have no notion of where they began. And so to thank everyone whose work has found its way into its pages would be impossible.

But there are some whose names I know well. First, my thanks to the lady who has done more than any other to bring together all those who love herbs—from their far-flung farms, their workshops, and potting sheds, their kitchens and their patio gardens—and made them into a group we all refer to as "the Potpourri Family." Phyllis Shaudys, through her newsletter, *Potpourri From Herbal Acres*, keeps us all in touch and gives us a way to share our discoveries, our triumphs, and our ideas about herbs.

To the members and officers of my own New Hampshire Herb Society, which includes many members far from New Hampshire's borders, a special thanks for sharing their secrets of growing glorious gardens in our less-than-kind climate. This group gathers each May at the Canterbury Shaker Village for an Herb Festival that draws visitors from all over the country, but for most of the year we know each other through an excellent newsletter. Through it, I have learned a great deal from my fellow members.

It was at one of the Canterbury festivals that I first met Betsy Williams, the remarkable creator of herbal weddings and herb wreaths. Just a few minutes with Betsy provides a month's supply of inspiration and energy, and I am grateful for her contagious enthusiasm and encouragement.

My appreciation also to a lady I have never met, but have known through our sporadic correspondence of many years. Bertha Reppert of Rosemary House in Mechanicsburg, Pennsylvania, is a prolific writer whose books and booklets contain fascinating information and fresh ideas. Like Betsy, her energy is super-human. Each of these people is part of this book and I can't imagine having written it without them.

Closer to home, my endless thanks to my Mother, Dee Radcliffe, and daughter, Julie Rogers, for their recipes, which I have used throughout the book. And to Lura and Tim who joined them in typing the manuscript. Knowing the four of them, I strongly suspect that they improved it considerably as they typed.

Contents

CHAPTER 1

Growing, Cultivating, and Harvesting Fresh Herbs

Why Fresh Herbs?

There are so many recipes, crafts, and projects that use dried herbs that one might easily ask, "Why grow fresh herbs? It seems that all there is to do with them is wait until they dry!" But to work only with dried herbs is to know only a fraction of the joy of herbs.

The delicate flavor and aroma of a sprig of lemon balm crowning a glass of iced tea, a fresh herbal bouquet alive and fragrant on the table, lavender wands, a sprig of fresh tarragon tucked into the cavity of a trout before it is grilled, heads of green dill seeds in a jar of crisp pickles—all of these and so many more recipes and crafts require freshly picked herbs.

Beyond the pleasures of using fresh herbs is the enjoyment of growing them: artemisia glowing in the moonlight, lemon balm fragrant in the midday sun, salad burnet shining a vivid green against the first snow. There is the comforting softness of lamb's ears, and the sense of accomplishment when a potted rosemary bursts forth into a froth of blue flowers in March.

The herb grower is a child of the ages, kin to Pliny and the monks of the Dark Ages. As we plant our seeds we sow with housewives of old, and with the women who came on the first ships to America, a few treasured seeds and cuttings tucked in their meager baggage. We tread woodland paths with native Americans and well-clipped garden paths with Queen Elizabeth I.

Tidy boxwood encloses beds in this shaded woodland herb garden.

We are children of the world as well, for herbs are a common language nearly everywhere. When our mutual poor French failed us, an herb seller in a remote village of Togo, West Africa took me by the hand to a nearby display of vegetables to show me which one to cook a particular herb with. On a craggy mountainside in Portugal, a tiny lady dressed in black told me by gesture and a mimicked cough that they use the wild horehound that grows there just as we do.

Mayan women in the highlands of Guatemala; Zulus in the street markets of Durban, South Africa; and Paris chefs, formidable in their toques, have discussed their herbs with me through the barriers of spoken

Opposite page: In a moderate climate lavender spreads into neat, attractive clumps and blooms in fragrant spikes of tiny purple flowers.

Lemon balm's uses are many and ancient—as medicine, tea, wood polish, and simply to lift the gardener's spirits.

The Cloisters, in Fort Tryon Park, New York, has one of North America's few authentic monastic gardens. Here, herbs and small fruit trees combine in a courtyard.

language, just as my friend Rita in Verona taught me to season baby artichokes with just enough basil, when the only common words we shared were *bon giorno* and *vino*.

Wherever we look, through the dimensions of time or distance, there are herbs—they are like old friends found in the pages of history or met far from home. Last year I stood amid the deserted ruins of a hill fort in Portugal, abandoned by its builders nearly 4,000 years ago. Archaeologists know from the artifacts that they had come from Italy, about 2,500 B.C. Abundant among the broken walls were beautiful, fragrant herbs, their roots between the stones, their leaves perfuming the air as I walked among them.

I have stood amid the rich fragrance of the fields of Norfolk lavender and walked the paths of the physician's garden at Padua, admired the sculptured knot gardens of Hampton Court, and shopped for fresh tarragon in the markets of Provence. In well-cared for gardens and in wild and deserted places where ancient peoples once led their everyday lives, I felt a strong kinship with the world and all its history, a kinship that the knowledge of herbs can bring.

The lore of herbs is almost as compelling as their scents and flavors, which is why there are so many myths, stories, and legends tucked, like pressed herbs, among the pages of this book. Herbs have been the subject of diaries, discourses, letters, and books almost since mankind developed ways of recording history. We can trace them to the Ebers Papyrus, a medical work of 1,500 B.C., and through the Dark Ages in carefully preserved monastic records; through the Ren-

aissance and later with the great diarists and early botanists of the time, and into the modern era in family receipt books and plantation records, and the meticulous diaries of the Shakers.

In the days before modern medicine, herbs were almost the only cure or relief for ailments, and their medicinal and household uses were passed carefully from one generation to the next. Some herbal remedies

were simply old wives' tales (or old physicians' tales), but others were based on the actual healing qualities of the plants. Many of these, such as the soothing horehound and the calming chamomile, are still in use today. So are many of the fragrant and cosmetic uses, and while we may not believe that sage in our garden makes us wise or immortal, we still use rosewater for hand cream and lavender to keep our linens fresh.

Herb or 'erb?

While we can talk of herbs even with those with whom we share no common language, we cannot agree among English speaking peoples on how to pronounce the word. In most parts of the United States it is "'erb," with a few New Englanders using the British "herb" with the "h" pronounced.

There is ample linguistic history on either side of this long-standing disagreement. With the Norman invasion of England in 1066 there came many changes to the Anglo-Saxon language, at least as it was spoken by the aristocracy. Words such as "honor" (*honeur*) and "hour" (*heure*) entered the English language at the same time as "herb," and the "h" has never been pronounced on either of them. But "herb" derived from "*herbe*," which although based on the Latin "*herba*," was spelled both "*herbe*" and "*erbe*" in old French. Researchers at the Brooklyn Botanic Garden in New York tell us that until 1475 the word was spelled and pronounced "'erb." Early in the next century the "h"

France and England are known as the home of the finest lavenders. Here, neat rows of lavender grow on a commercial farm in Provence, France, where they are harvested and used in perfume.

from Latin was reattached in spelling, but not pronounced for another three hundred years.

Since then, well-spoken British have become conscious of sounding like Cockneys, "dropping h's everywhere," and use the "h" in "herb," although not, for some reason, in "hour" or "honor." They say "a herb," but still use expressions such as "an 'istoric occasion," indicating by the use of "an" that the "h" was purposely dropped. (A Cockney, presumably, would say "a 'erb" or "a 'istoric occasion.")

So, feel assured in saying whichever rolls more easily from your tongue, remembering that you have 'istory firmly on your side!

Ideas From Early Herb Gardens

We owe most of our knowledge of early herb gardens to the records and accounts of monks, in whose gardens were cultivated the plants for food, medicine, and church festivals. The monks took the design of Roman atrium gardens and blended it into the monastic cloister, a square or rectangular enclosure cut into quarters by intersecting paths, with a fountain or water tank in the center; this lent itself to formal, symmetrical arrangements. The infirmary gardens were composed of close-set beds near the infirmary walls, and enclosed by a hedge or a fence. Most often there was a kitchen garden as well, and pot herbs and vegetables growing together in rows.

These basic garden forms remained, with some refinements and changes, for hundreds of years. With the Renaissance came an increased interest in exotic plants and a decline in the symbolic and mystical importance of the plants grown. Some of the old beliefs about the supernatural powers of plants fell so far out of favor that they were associated with witchcraft.

During the seventeenth century, useful plants began to be separated from ornamentals, with herbs, flowers, fruit, and vegetables all divided into separate plots and only the cottage gardens of the lower classes remained as one entity. Mixed cottage gardens enjoyed a revival in the late nineteenth century, when Victorian gardens were a riot of different herbs and flowers grown together. Recent interest in herbs has led to a revival of the herb garden as a separate plot, and of ornamental arrangements such as knot gardens. Like

Above top: Italian, or flat-leaf, parsley was grown in the earliest gardens and is still a favorite of cooks and gardeners. *Above bottom:* Lady's mantle is included in todays herb gardens for its biblical connections and the beauty of its widespreading foliage.

Right: Cut stones can be set above ground level to form the supporting wall for raised herb beds, and they are more attractive than wood. *Far right:* Even informal herb gardens such as this one at Pickety Place, in Mason, New Hampshire, have an air of order about them.

the pronunciation, the layout of herbs in the garden is a matter of personal taste, and whichever design you choose for their arrangement, you will have historic precedent.

The medieval garden in Europe showed the first signs of the influence of traditional Oriental pleasure gardens. First activated in castle walls, then in the palace grounds of the aristocracy, these small walled gardens had arbors for shade and benches for relaxation. Their emphasis was on plants that were fragrant, beautiful, or both. Small trees were trained to espalier against walls or were clipped to topiary shapes as they had been in Roman gardens centuries earlier. Arrangements were symmetrical.

During the Renaissance, the layout remained symmetrical, but instead of walled enclosures, the gardens were separated by hedges, arbors, or balustrades. The Italian influence swept across Europe, with larger gardens, sweeping vistas, and box hedges outlining elaborate curved and circular beds. Ornaments abounded: classical statues, sundials, fountains, and gatehouses. In fifteenth-century England, knot gardens in intricate designs reminiscent of Moorish tiles became popular. These gardens were divided by low hedges of fragrant plants, such as lavender, boxwood, thyme, savory, and germander.

In 1545 the first of the great botanic "physic" gardens was established in Padua. Botanists began to classify plants in earnest, and many of the great herbals were published in the seventeenth century. The most famous of these, Gerard's *Herbal,* was published in the last years of the sixteenth century, and even today remains a classic on the uses, horticulture, and

Knot gardens are at their best when seen from above, from a terrace, or from a window, where the full design is visible.

lore of herbs, bringing together all the various botanical disciplines.

Plants found in the New World were collected, studied, and incorporated into Old World gardens, while the colonists of North America learned their uses from native Americans. The eighteenth-century Swedish botanist Linnaeus was busy classifying these and European species according to the binomial system we still use. Early in the nineteenth century, the first Shaker medicinal garden was established in America and members of this sect became the first seedsmen, making vegetable and herb seeds available in packets much as they are today.

Always pragmatic, Americans scorned formal ornamental gardens in favor of the practical: They planted herbs and vegetables together in gardens convenient to the back door. At the same time in England, garden styles became more and more elaborate with dramatic beds of brilliant color, moving away from the subtle, inconspicuous colors of herbs.

It is from these traditions that today's gardener may draw inspiration; today's garden fashions are eclectic and imaginative, with no set rules. So, in planning your own herb garden, whether a front border, a back-yard patch, a city patio, or a sprawling meadow, choose those plants you like and put them where they will grow best, in an arrangement that pleases you.

Herbs and everlastings are combined with ornamental flowers in this mid-eighteenth century formal garden, recreated in Old Sturbridge Village, Sturbridge, Massachusetts.

Planning a Garden

Although fencing is rarely used in herbs beds, a border of bent cane provides some protection to plants in heavy traffic areas.

The first thing to consider when planning a garden is its location. Because of circumstances such as space and exposure, you may have no choice on where your garden grows. In that case, make the most of what you have by planting herbs suited to that environment. If you do have the luxury of several different locations, you can fill each with plants adapted to particular conditions. The herbs listed in "An Album of Herbs" suggest those which thrive in shade and arid ground. Herbs that tolerate partial shade will usually do better if they receive full sun, but can be grown in an area shaded for part of the day with a correspondingly lower production. Herbs that thrive in dry soil will do well in a wet summer as long as they have good drainage

and don't stand in soggy soil. About the only herb that can tolerate wet feet is mint, which can withstand almost anything.

Once perennial herb beds are established and annual herbs are not needed to fill in spaces, many gardeners prefer to plant their annuals in rows with the vegetables, where weeds can be controlled by using a Rototiller. This is especially useful for those who grow a lot of basil for pesto or coriander for its leaves. Sorrel, arugula, and dill are also usually grown in the vegetable garden. Perennial flower beds are a good setting for most perennial herbs, especially tall or blooming ones like yarrow and tansy. Many have showy blossoms, and those that don't often have foliage that is attractive in shape, color, or texture.

Both nasturtiums and calendula are perfectly at home in the annual border, as is perilla, which is grown as an ornamental in many of the beautiful public gardens of Portugal. Opal basil, if it is kept bushy with regular pinching, works well too.

Garden Designs

If you are just beginning to grow herbs, or if you are fairly new at gardening, it is tempting to try to grow everything at once. You long to grow each plant you see or smell or read about, and it seems impossible to narrow your selections to just a few. It's even worse if you have visited a few well-established gardens and seen how lovely they are with their full clumps and cascading abundance.

The first thing to remember is that most herbs take a season or two, or even more, to spread into those nicely shaped mounds. The second is that herbs can be moved. Instead of planning a half-acre garden with brick paths and statuary, which would take years to build and a decade more to fill, begin with a small layout and alternate spreading perennial herbs with annual and biennial herbs, so that there is room for growth but still a good variety of plants.

When planning any design, always take height into consideration, since taller plants will often shade smaller plants and inhibit their growth. In addition to shading, some larger plants multiply so quickly that they choke out the less vigorous ones planted nearby.

Flowering plants of different heights and colors can be mixed for an effective border as in this California garden.

HERBS BY HEIGHT

Tall herbs: artemisia, bay, dill, fennel, lovage, roses, sage, tansy

Medium height: lavender, lemon balm, pineapple mint, tarragon

Ground covers: chamomile, lemon thyme, violets, woodruff

Herbs that spread quickly: artemisia, bee balm, spearmint (first prize!), tansy

© Terri Wright

A Border Garden

The easiest design of all is a simple border garden: a rectangle about three feet wide set against a wall or fence. Lest you think this isn't really a proper herb garden, it is the design used at Westminster Abbey in London and in the Abbey in Hampshire, England. There are no paths to worry with. Tall plants go in back, short ones in front, and middle-sized in between. This is a good garden in which to play with color combinations: Tall background plants could include gray sage and silver artemisia alternating with bright green and yellow yarrow or tansy, and feathery copper fennel, perhaps highlighted with bee balm.

The middle-size plants could include lavender, lovage, pineapple sage, calendula, basil, pot marjoram, lemon balm, or clove pinks. Along the front, the shorter plants, depending on the size and color of the others, could be parsley, chive, chervil, violets, thyme, winter savory, or nasturtiums.

By alternating perennials with annuals and biennials, you will have a first-year garden that is slightly busy, but at least not empty and sparse. By the second year, your perennials will have spread enough to fill in some of the spaces, but you will still have room to tuck a few annuals in among them.

A Formal Herb Garden

The easiest "formal" herb bed to build and begin is a simple square bisected diagonally by two paths. This forms four triangles and provides easy access to all parts of the beds. Each of these triangles offers ample space for at least four plants. Put a tall or spreading herb in the center of each, an annual or biennial at each of the center corners, and smaller perennials at the outside corners. Thyme, lavender, and mint in a large sunken pot, and lemon balm, bee balm, or chive are good center choices.

Tarragon, winter savory, scented geranium, salad

Here, opal basil is used with stunning effect in a border planting.

A sundial is a popular centerpiece for herb gardens, especially round ones.

Formal knot gardens depend on small compact herbs that form close hedges.

burnet, small sages, rosemary (except in the south, where it grows quite large), oregano, lamb's ear, fennel, costmary, clove pink, or chamomile are good plants for the outside corners. If the garden is fairly small, the center plants may soon fill the beds, at which time you should stop planting the annuals. You can either prune back the roots of the center plants to make room for the more upright corner perennials, or you can move these to another garden.

Tall or rapidly spreading plants such as yarrow, artemisia, or tansy are not for these gardens unless the beds are quite large. In that case the beds can be bisected with other paths (see diagrams 3 and 7 on page 21), or a large circular or square bed can be placed in the center (as in diagrams 2, 5, or 7 on page 21). If you begin with a small square, other identical gardens can be added, either in a row or forming another large square made up of four smaller ones.

Knot Gardens

Knot gardens are more difficult to grow in cold climates since the most successful ones depend on boxwood, which does not winter well in northern zones, and doesn't form the desirable lush, full growth even in some of the central zones. The same is true of lavender, the other standby in manicured hedges, although it will survive farther north than will boxwood. But southern gardeners can combine these two plants for beautiful contrast, or can replace one or the other with either germander or rosemary. Many knot

Small wooden boards can hold a raised herb bed and provide a tidy border for the garden.

gardens only use outlining hedges and fill in the space between them with white gravel or mulch, but others fill in the sections with full, low-growing plants such as thyme or lamb's ear. Knot gardens need to be kept clipped, usually three times each growing season. They are not good choices for very dry climates.

Before beginning to plant your knot garden, mark the design on the ground with garden lime. This serves two purposes: First, it clearly defines the beds where plantings need to be made; second, it balances the pH, which should be fairly alkaline for most of the hedge-forming plants. If your soil is already alkaline, mark the design using a sprinkling of fine white sand poured through a paper funnel.

Herbs can be grown in rows in a vegetable or flower garden, or inter-planted with vegetables.

The Kitchen Garden

While it is more fun to have a garden just for herbs, it is often more practical and/or more ornamental to grow them with vegetables and flowers. The classic cottage garden (English), or kitchen garden (American), and the French *potager jardin* combine culinary herbs with flowers or vegetables. The kitchen garden puts all the ingredients for dinner close at hand and gives the gardener the added advantage of companion planting. This gardening method relies on the natural insecticidal and soil-enriching qualities of herbs to help vegetables perform better. Garlic or chive, for example, planted among carrots repels carrot flies. Chamomile has long been known as "the plant doctor," since an ailing plant will revive when chamomile is planted close to it. The list of companion plants found below can help you plan your kitchen garden,

COMPANION PLANTS

Savory—Green Beans
Basil—Tomatoes
Nasturtium and Thyme—Cabbage
Garlic—Roses
Tansy—Cucumbers
Nasturtium—Beans
Garlic, Chive, or Coriander—Carrots
Horseradish—Potatoes
Nasturtium—Squash
Borage—Strawberries

which is usually laid out in simple rows or raised beds. Only a few plants of each vegetable are grown in the backdoor kitchen garden, but herbs and vegetables can just as easily be mixed in a full-size garden.

center or at one end. A potted bay or rosemary can serve the same purpose, giving a dimension of height, as can a raised bed in the center filled with tall artemisia or yarrow. A bay or rosemary trained as a topiary is a lovely centerpiece for a smaller garden.

Miscellaneous Garden Designs

There are many other designs for gardens, most of which can be adapted to fit into any available space. For an area that slopes at one end, give a sense of depth with a winding path, perhaps of large stepping stones for even greater space. These curved paths fool the eye into seeing more space than is actually there, a secret of the tiny Japanese gardens which appear much bigger than they are. (Diagrams 1 and 4 both use this trick.)

The illusion of space can also be achieved by using different shades of green and by limiting the number of bright blossoms. Taller plants in the rear and along the edges give an illusion of depth. In a small space, paving stones set a bit apart serve a practical as well as a visual purpose, since they cover less of the available space than a solid path. Low-growing chamomile or thyme, woodruff or violets can grow in the spaces in between the flag stones, and the stones will provide a perch as you work in the garden.

Any of these designs can be adapted to fit a different shape or size by repeating them, elongating them, rounding their corners to form a circle, or simply lopping off a side.

Larger gardens often have a focal point such as a sundial, statue, bee skep, bench, or arbor, either in the

Herb Garden Designs

Special Gardens to Enjoy

Once you have grown a few herbs, you may want to plant a garden with a special theme, using herbs associated with your hobbies or interests, such as a biblical, historical, potpourri, or tea garden. Those of literary bent might want to plant a garden of herbs mentioned by poets or those to which Shakespeare referred. Nature lovers will enjoy a garden of plants to attract bees, butterflies, or hummingbirds; or, if you have a porch or patio where you sit on a summer evening, you might surround it with a moonlight garden of pale green and gray herbs.

A potpourri garden of scented herbs could have an old-fashioned rosebush in the center, or a central bed could be circular and planted to look like a nosegay. Tufts of clove pink bordered in white-edged silver thyme will give the appearance of lace surrounding rosebuds. Sweet and spicy fragrant plants such as rosemary, lemon verbena, scented geraniums, mints, lemon grass, lemon balm, lavender, chamomile, and bay are good for this garden.

Two of the world's great botanical gardens, the Brooklyn Botanic Garden in New York City and Kirstenbosch Gardens in Capetown, South Africa, have gardens designed especially for the blind. Markers are in braille and the plants are grown in raised beds set on walls to put their fragrance within easy reach. Such a garden could be used as a border atop a retaining wall or terrace, where it would be easy to bury your nose in plants without bending over.

There is no better garden than this one for a bench where you can pause for a moment to enjoy the fragrances. Such a scented corner with a seat might be set against a bank where fragrant flowers could grow at nose level behind the bench, or roses planted at each end of it. A fragrant shrub such as mock orange, or an arbor behind or over the bench could offer some shade.

These quiet corners of repose are also a good way to reclaim some unsightly area, such as the corner where house and garage meet, or where your property abuts the back of a neighbor's fence. Walls or fences can be covered with flowering vines such as trumpet creeper, honeysuckle, or climbing roses.

In choosing plants, look for a variety of scents, not

© Rogers Assoc.

Bay is seen growing along stone walls in Old Sturbridge Village, Sturbridge, Massachusetts.

Opposite page, left: Brick paths separate beds of mixed herbs in this more formal herb garden. *Opposite page, right:* Bee skeps are a traditional centerpiece for the herb garden. Although these are not often used to house bees, they are a popular accent.

HERBS FOR COLOR

Blue: blue balsam mint, borage, lavender, violets
Bright green: dill, fennel, golden sage, lovage
Deep green: box, germander, rosemary, winter savory
Orange: calendula, nasturtium
Pink: chive, clove pink, pot marjoram, rose, saffron, yarrow
Purple: bronze fennel, opal basil, perilla, purple sage
Red: bee balm, pineapple sage
Silver-gray: artemisia, costmary, horehound, lamb's ears, lavender, sage
White: garlic chive, woodruff
Yellow: chamomile, costmary, tansy, yarrow

just the sweet, heavy ones. Lemon verbena and lavender are invigorating, while lemon balm and chamomile are soothing. Plant chamomile or thyme between paving stones. Clove pinks add a spicy fragrance, and scented geraniums can be set in pots, to be brought indoors for winter, refreshing your home with their scented leaves.

A tea garden could be planted with mint, bee balm, catnip, chamomile, sage, costmary, and scented geraniums. It, too, might contain a bench or a wrought-iron patio table and chairs, just large enough for tea-time. In this case, you could add an arbor of climbing roses and a border of nasturtiums to use in your tea sandwiches.

Throughout this book are quotes from Shakespeare and other poets. These are a good place to find ideas for

a Shakespearean or poets' garden, which could be an appropriate variation on the Elizabethan knot garden.

A biblical garden could include those plants mentioned in the bible or those known to grow in the Holy Land today. Biblical scholars do not agree on the plants actually meant by some of the biblical references,

however, since names of plants have changed since then. For example, some scholars believe that the bitter herbs of Passover are sorrel, chicory, and endive eaten as a salad, not horehound and other "herbs" in the narrower modern sense. And the anise of Jesus's rebuke of the Pharisees is now commonly thought to be an early mistranslation of dill. So that list would read "mint, dill, and cumin."

Another approach might be to grow herbs associated with the Virgin Mary or other saints. Rosemary, cost-mary, lady's mantle, lady's bedstraw, and calendula (pot marigold) were all named for Mary, while laven-der, bay, chive, horehound, rose, violet, sage, woodruff, tansy, and thyme have all been associated with saints or Christian observance.

Brick paths make neat edgings and help control spreading herbs and grass intrusion.

Gardening is a hobby every member of the family can en-joy.

Planting Your Herb Garden

Once you have decided where to put your herbs and how you want to arrange them, there is one more step before you can actually put plants in the ground. Although it is sometimes skipped over by hurried gardeners, preparation of the soil is very important to the success of any garden.

Unless your herbs are going into an established flower bed or vegetable garden, you will need to re-move all grass, weeds, roots, and other growing things from the soil. If you are putting herbs where grass has grown, do *not* Rototill the lawn into the soil. Instead, remove the turf (grass and roots) in squares made with the sharp edge of a spade. This removes the entire growing layer and prevents existing roots from filling your herb bed with persistent grass. These cut blocks of turf can be reset and kept well watered to replace a section of poor lawn elsewhere. The surrounding lawn will reinvade the cut-out area, so it is a good idea to use an edging of metal or plastic that is simply pushed into the soil along the edges of the bed. Push it into the ground until its top is even with the soil, so it won't show.

Having protected your bed from encroachment, you now need to prepare the soil by digging it up and loosening it to a depth of six to eight inches (twenty-one to twenty-eight centimeters). This is easy to do with a spade or a gardening fork. As you work, remove any roots or runners (see page 30 for more information on runners) that might remain, and dig out any deep-rooted weeds such as dandelions or chicory (both well-respected herbs, but ones you might not want in your new garden!). Remove rocks and, if your soil is sandy or has heavy clay in it, work in some well-composted manure or other organic material. The ideal soil for herbs is sandy enough to provide good drainage, but organic enough to hold moisture, nutrients, and air.

Because so many herbs grow natively in the sparse, lean soil of the dry Mediterranean hillsides, a myth has gained acceptance that they actually do best in these conditions. The fact is, like any other plant, herbs will respond best when treated well. It is true that overfertilizing causes many of them to produce less flavorful leaves, but good growing conditions in a moderately loamy soil will produce fragrant, flavorful herbs that are also healthy plants and attractive additions to the garden. A few herbs have special requirements for pH balance, but this can be adjusted by "digging in" (mixing into the soil before planting) wood ashes (alkaline) or peat moss (acid) around the individual plants.

The ideal soil texture is crumbly and slightly granular, with spaces between the soil particles and tiny bits of organic matter. It neither compacts into modeling-clay consistency nor runs in a fine stream like sand through an hourglass.

The nutrient content of your soil can be determined by having a soil test done by your County Extension office. This will also tell you the pH balance, and since most herbs do best in soil that is neutral to

HERBS FOR SPECIAL GROWING CONDITIONS

Herbs that thrive in shade: peppermint, spearmint, violets, woodruff

Herbs that thrive in partial shade: anise hyssop, costmary, lovage, saffron, salad burnet, spearmint, tarragon, violets

Herbs that tolerate partial shade: chervil, chive, mint, nasturtium, parsley, sorrel

Herbs that thrive in dry soil: artemisia, chamomile, catnip, fennel, horehound, lavender, marjoram, oregano, rosemary, sage, tansy, thyme, winter savory

slightly alkaline, you may want to work in some wood ashes or agricultural lime if your soil is acid. The test will also tell if your soil is low in any of the three main nutrients (nitrogen, phosphorous, and potassium), and you can add these by choosing a fertilizer rich in what your soil lacks.

A little time and energy spent on the soil will repay you amply during many years of gardening. Healthy, weed-free soil not only produces better plants, but it resists disease. Also, free of underground runners or weed grasses, your soil will grow only those weeds whose seeds land on top if it, and are easily removed as tiny seedlings.

Most beginning herb gardeners purchase their pe-

The rich purple color of some sages can be used to beautiful effect as massed plantings in a larger garden.

rennial plants from nurseries or use those shared by friends. Although you might later wish to raise your own perennials from seed, these are very slow to establish and often take two years before they are more than a spindly, single-stemmed plant. You are better off saving your windowsill space for the seedlings of annual plants.

In purchasing plants from a nursery, look for those that are healthy and "field-grown" if possible; these will be in large pots and have well-developed roots. While smaller greenhouse plants may do well, you know that field-hardy plants are suited to the rigors of outdoor life. Some herb nurseries will simply take a shovel into the garden and dig you a clump, while others have pots of field-grown plants already dug up.

Either of these types is ready to plant immediately (freshly dug plants must be planted at once, before the newly bared rootlets dry out).

For tender perennials or those which have been propagated in the greenhouse, look for sturdy, well-branched plants with strong stems and good root growth. A very gentle tug on the stem right above the

STRAWBERRY JARS

These attractive terra-cotta pots with a series of shelflike openings are ideal for herbs, although they are a bit more tricky to care for because of the layers of plants and the tendency of unglazed pots to dry out from all sides at once. Be sure that the plants you choose are compatible and that none is invasive. Mint would be a poor choice unless you want an entire potful.

Insert a length of perforated plastic pipe or a cylinder of wire screen down the center of the pot and fill it with perlite. This is to keep the water supply even. Fill in the potting mixture around it, and insert small plants in the little shelved holes. Thyme, coriander (for its leaves), winter savory, and chives all do well in these. For the top, choose a full, upright plant such as parsley, which will finish off your arrangement beautifully. Larger strawberry jars work better than smaller ones since they hold more soil and are slower to dry out. Be sure to turn the pot regularly so all sides get sun.

Single wooden edgings keep gravel paths and garden soil separate in the herb garden.

soil line will tell you if they have just been potted or if they have developed a good root system in their pot. The risk of losing newly potted plants is much higher, and although you may be willing to try your luck with one in order to obtain a hard-to-find variety, you should be prepared to give it special care.

Tender greenhouse plants will need to "harden off" for about a week before they are planted outside. Water them well and set them outdoors for about two hours in the late afternoon, extending the time by about an hour each day for two or three days, then by two hours a day. Bring them in at night for the first week, then leave them out, still potted, for two nights before finally transplanting to the garden. Be sure to check them for water on hot, sunny, or windy days, since the pots hold very little moisture and the plants shouldn't dry out. If the day is windy, be sure the plants are in a protected place until they have stronger stems.

When they have become used to outdoor life, dig holes about twice the depth and diameter of the pot and mix in some rich humus or potting soil. Fill the hole with water mixed with a small amount of liquid fertilizer. Stir this rich mud well and make a depression in its center large enough for the roots of your new plant. If it has become pot-bound, loosen its roots slightly, holding the plant over the hole.

The best time to transplant is on a cloudy, fairly warm day, when plants will suffer the least shock. On a sunny day, transplant late in the afternoon or very early in the morning. Check the plants during the hottest part of the first few days, giving them a little shade if they seem to be drooping badly.

Herb seedlings on display at a garden center. Be sure seedlings are strongly rooted in their pots before purchasing.

Starting Annuals From Seed

Start the seeds in long plastic trays which are divided into inch-wide rows, and sit suspended in deeper, solid plastic trays that hold water. Or, if you are starting only a few plants, use individual peat pots or small flower pots. Use a sterile starting medium, like Jiffy-Mix, which is fine and light in texture, holding necessary moisture without becoming soggy and drowning

Seed-Starting Method: *Top left:* Fill the seed flat with soil. *Top right:* Sow seeds in the flat. *Bottom left:* Cover the seeds with more soil. *Bottom right:* Soon, herbs will begin to sprout.

cover the seeds with as much as a half inch (1.75 centimeters) of starter mix. Set the seed trays in the solid trays you have half-filled with lukewarm water. Be sure to label each section so you can tell the seedlings apart. Set the trays in a warm place where they will get as much sun as possible.

When the seedlings are about one inch (3.5 centimeters) tall, move them to individual pots, carefully separating the roots. Put two or three in each pot, unless the seeds are very delicate or their germination poor. When this is the case, it is best to use up a pot for a weak seedling than to waste a possible plant. When the plants are well rooted and have developed true leaves, cut off all but the strongest plant in each pot, clipping with scissors instead of pulling, to avoid disturbing the roots of the remaining plant.

By the time they are well established in individual pots, these annuals may be hardened off and planted in the garden whenever the weather conditions are right, just as you would for purchased plants.

Once herbs are established in the garden, they are quite easy to care for. Weeds can be removed easily if they are pulled before they have a chance to develop serious roots. Pruning is not usually a problem with cooking herbs since the constant removal of sprigs for kitchen use encourages fuller, bushier growth. When woody plants such as lavender begin to look straggly, or if they form one single stem without side branches, they can be pruned back, but be careful not to remove flower stems before the flowers have formed.

Although herbs are rarely troubled by pests or diseases, an occasional attack may occur. Herbs can often

tiny sprouts. A fine-grained starter mix is also important when it comes time to separate the tender roots and move them to individual pots.

Pour the dry soil mix into the long rows, filling each within a quarter inch (.9 centimeter) of the top. Shake the trays gently to settle, but not pack the mix, then add more if needed. Tap seeds gently onto the soil, trying to avoid clumping them, and spread with your fingers until they are about eight to ten to the inch, three to four to a pot. Since the seeds of some herbs are tiny, it is almost impossible to get them evenly spread, and it is not necessary to try.

According to the light needs of each type of herb—read the packets carefully to learn what these are—

protect each other by providing natural insect repellants. A clove or two of garlic mixed in the blender with a pint of water makes a quick spray for aphids and other insects. If you are growing costmary, throw a handful of its leaves into this insect-repelling mixture for extra protection. A few drops of liquid dishwashing soap make this solution stick to the leaves when the mixture is sprayed on. Indoor plants, unless they have full sun all day, tend to become "leggy" and need to be pruned fairly often to keep them full and tidy. But since the purpose of having them indoors is to have them handy to use fresh, they are normally pruned by the cook.

If the soil of potted plants shows signs of mildew, put the plant in the sun and allow it to dry out a little.

Or treat it with a dose of chamomile spray used to prevent "damping off" of seedlings (see page 64).

If you plan to move the plants outdoors again in the spring, be sure to harden them off as you would newly grown plants, before transplanting. If you plan to grow herbs indoors all year round, they will be healthier if you can give them some time outdoors in the summer, on a balcony or patio or in a sunny window box.

Many gardeners who have plenty of land for herb beds still choose to grow herbs in pots on a patio just for their decorative value and the convenience of having them nearby. Others grow them there because it is the only available outdoor space for an herb garden. Whatever the reason, herbs adapt well to being grown outdoors in pots, tubs, and planters. Those such as

The traditional quartet of parsley, sage, rosemary, and thyme are together here in large pots.

Most public herb gardens, such as this one at the Cincinnati Nature Center, have easily visible labels to identify plants.

thyme, prostrate rosemary, and nasturtium, which cascade over the sides of the pot, are particularly attractive. Others can become imposing shrubs.

Sharing Your Riches

One of the great pleasures of herb gardening is being able to share your favorite plants with friends. Herbs are propagated in a variety of ways, much the same as other garden plants: runners, layering, stem cuttings, and seeds. Once your plants are well enough established you can enlarge your own gardens with new plants you've propagated, or you can trade these with other gardeners for new varieties.

Runners

The easiest plants to propagate are those which form runners, either above or underground, from which new plants grow. Peppermint is a good example of an herb that spreads by aboveground runners. In fact, it does so much of the work for you that your conscience may not let you claim any of the credit! It sends forth its runners as lateral stems that put down roots every few inches and grow new plants at each of these roots. All you need to do is cut the runner and scoop up the new plant. Or you can move the runner and anchor it with a stone in the direction you would like the new plants to grow.

Like spearmint, peppermint can withstand shade. Here it is used as a ground cover under a tree.

Basil is a very versatile kitchen herb.

Other members of the mint family send runners underground and you will see new plants begin to grow in more or less straight lines radiating from the parent. To move these, simply break the runners with a trowel and dig up the new plants. Spearmint carries this propagation to belligerent extremes, as you will note in "An Album of Herbs" (see page 42).

Layering

Layering involves almost the same process as runners, but instead of a runner, the outside woody stems of some plants will set down roots wherever they remain against moist soil for an extended period of time. Thyme, winter savory, tarragon, and lavender are some of the woody perennials that can be propagated this way, but they will often need a little help from you. First, find outer branches that can easily bend down to soil level, and strip off a few leaves two or three inches (seven to ten centimeters) back from the first branches. If there are no leaves there, scratch the bark slightly with the blade of a trowel to break its surface. Push the stripped or scraped area into the loosened soil and lay a rock on top of it to hold it down. It is even more effective to anchor it to the ground with a wire hairpin. Be sure the soil is kept moist, then let the plant do the rest. If this is done in the spring, new plants will be ready in late summer, but fall layering makes even stronger plants, which are ready to move when you rearrange your garden in the spring.

If you intend to pot the newly rooted plants to bring indoors for winter, swap them with your friends, or

Thyme's compact growth and tidy habit make it a popular border plant in an herb garden.

A countryside setting is the perfect backdrop for this garden of pink dianthus and other fragrant herbs.

donate them to plant sales, you can layer the stems directly into small pots sunk into the soil just to their rims. Anchor the branch to be layered directly into the soil in the pot, and when it is rooted, snip off the stem connecting it to the parent plant.

Mound layering often works better with stiffly upright plants like lavender. Instead of bringing the stems down to the ground, you mound the soil up around the base of the plant, burying several stems. In the spring, you can carefully separate each of the rooted stems into a new plant, cutting it off below the new roots, but above the main root crown of the parent plant.

Many plants expand by growing larger from the base, with new stems rising from a central root clump. To divide these, simply dig up a clump and carefully pull or cut it into sections, or use a trowel to chop off outer sections while the rest of the plant is still in the ground. Replant as you would a transplant.

Stem Cuttings

Stem cuttings require a little more care and attention, but are the best way to propagate many plants; rosemary is especially suitable for this method. These cuttings are taken in the spring or early summer from the soft new stem growth. They can be taken at any time of the year, but cuttings rooted in the spring have a better chance of becoming established in the ground or in pots before winter.

Water the plant well about six hours before making

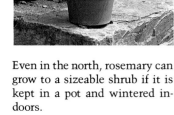

© Rogers Assoc.

Even in the north, rosemary can grow to a sizeable shrub if it is kept in a pot and wintered indoors.

cuttings. Choose a piece of new growth (those shoots with soft stems that have not become woody), three to six inches (eleven to twenty-one centimeters) long, and make a clean cut with a razor blade or sharp knife (scissors or clippers crush the stem). Cut the end at a slant to provide more surface for the roots to grow. If the cutting has been taken from a plant where you cannot make a careful knife cut, simply clip the end of the cutting at an angle afterward.

Dip the cut end into a rooting hormone, such as Jiffy Grow, to speed the formation of roots, and place the end in a small pot filled with a mixture of equal parts perlite and vermiculite, the two most important ingredients in potting soil as they are lightweight and water

I know a cheery woman
     And every time she calls
She leaves my carpets on the floor,
My pictures on the walls.

She doesn't steal my silver,
Or ask me for a loan,
She doesn't borrow my fountain pen,
She always brings her own.

But, show her in the garden
The treasures you have got,
And if you turn your head away,
She'll pinch the blooming lot!

Taken from the book *Herbs and Herb Gardens of Britain* by Elizabeth and Reginald Peplow, Exeter, England: Webb and Bower.

Like chamomile, thyme can be grown as a lawn, although it requires careful attention.

friends, even those some distance away. As long as they are kept moist, snips of tender new growth can travel for a few days and can even be enclosed in an envelope if wrapped in plastic with a damp tissue around the cut end. When they arrive, the ends should be freshly cut before planting in a rooting medium. Gardeners will often snip off sprigs of scented geraniums, lavender, or rosemary to share with visiting friends.

Seeds

Collecting seeds is a good way to propagate herbs such as salad burnet and garlic chives. In fact, if you don't collect the seeds from these, they will scatter and replant themselves. Wait for the seed heads to ripen and allow them to dry on the plant as much as possible. Then cut the heads off and allow them to dry completely on a screen. In most cases, these seeds can be planted directly in the garden, where they will grow the following year. Or you can store them in the freezer and plant them the next spring.

Clumps of purple violets will bloom in the early spring before many other herbs are out of the ground.

absorbent. Make a hole first with a stick or the blade of a table knife, then push the rooting medium back into place around the stem. Water well and allow the excess to drain out. Then cover the pot with an inverted, clear plastic drinking glass and place it in a window where it will get daylight but not direct sun. Keep the "soil" just moist, but don't allow the pot to sit in water. A temperature between 75°F and 85°F (22°C and 26°C) is optimum. After two weeks, carefully pull on the stem: If it releases easily, it has not begun to root, but if it offers a little resistance, roots have begun to form. When these are firmly anchored, you can carefully transplant them to potting soil and remove the plastic covers. Continue to water them well and treat them as you would newly transplanted seedlings.

Stem cuttings are an easy way to share plants with

Even small children can enjoy planting seeds and watching them grow into plants.

Putting Herbs to Bed

Many plants, such as chives and violets, die back to ground level each winter, springing up again the next year with no particular effort on your part. But others, such as lavender and winter savory, retain woody growth over the winter and form new leaves on these existing plants in the spring. If left untrimmed, woody stems are likely to form new spring growth at their outer tips, leaving bare, straggly center stems. These plants should be pruned back in the fall, but not so far back as to remove all the leaves, since these continue to support the plant until it is completely dormant. The root systems of these plants are fairly fragile and the alternate freezing and thawing of the ground breaks the tiny root hairs that the dormant plants depend on for nourishment and moisture in the spring.

After the ground has frozen, mulch woody herbs lightly with a layer of pine needles, salt hay, or clean straw. (Don't use stable straw, which contains high quantities of nitrogen. The last thing your plants need as they enter the winter months is more nitrogen.) Leaves are not a good mulch, since they pack down and hold too much moisture, which can damage the

Northern gardeners often extend their growing season by setting herbs outside in protected boxes that are covered at night, saving them from wind, beating rain, and spring frosts.

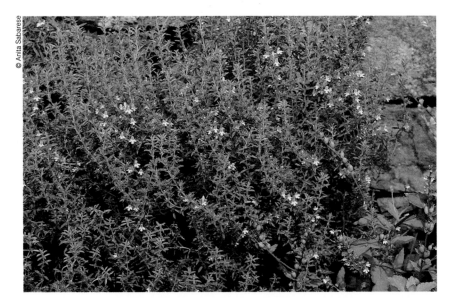

Winter savory will withstand even severe winters if it is pruned back in the fall and covered with pine boughs.

roots. Some gardeners fear that pine needles will add acidity to their soil, but this is not the case. In fact, pine trees thrive in acid soil, and tend to grow there, but they do not make the soil acid with their needles. In any event, the branches should be removed, and the ground raked in the spring before the needles can compost into the soil.

Before the vegetation on non-woody herbs dies back to the ground, mark their location with sticks or another durable marker. In the spring this will help you avoid digging them up by mistake as you clean out the beds for early planting.

In the spring, remove the mulch from woody perennials as the ground begins to thaw—about the time the first tulip leaves emerge. Clean up the perennial beds and tidy up any unwanted spreading growth in preparation for a new season.

Growing Herbs Indoors

While herbs are barely tamed outdoor plants by nature, several of them do quite well when grown indoors as long as they have the right location. The best possible scenario for successful indoor herb growing is a bay window over the kitchen sink on the south side of the house. Since very few people have that exact combination, the next best thing is to come as close as possible.

Sunlight at least half the day, high humidity, moderately low temperatures, ventilation, and good drainage

are the major requirements of potted herbs. Location, then, is the first key to success. Those homes that keep their thermostats at an energy-conscious level around 65°F (17°C) will have better plants than those with higher heat levels. A bay window is often the coolest spot in a room at night, but allows maximum daytime sunlight. The kitchen sink puts moisture in the air every time the hot water runs, so although the kitchen contains cooking oils in the air and higher temperatures than almost any other room in the

Many herbs can be grown indoors as long as they have the right conditions.

house, the humidity in that spot makes up for these other problems.

Nearly any spot in the house can be fitted with grow-lights if there isn't sufficient sunlight, or plants can be moved from place to place to take advantage of available light. Winter is by far the most difficult season for herbs indoors, both because of the dry air and because plants have a natural clock that tells them they should be dormant then. But in most climates, that is when gardeners want to bring herbs inside.

After location, the most important consideration is soil. Bringing a plant indoors in its garden soil is unwise, since with its roots constricted in a pot, the plant needs richer soil with maximum moisture retention. It does not need the soil-born fungus diseases and insects that garden soil carries with it.

There are excellent commercial potting soils available, or you can mix your own with equal parts of perlite, vermiculite, and peat moss with one tablespoon of ground eggshells added per quart of soil to counteract the acidity of the peat moss.

If planted in a pot that makes room for the long taproot, parsley can be lush and beautiful as a hanging plant.

HANGING BASKETS

Limited windowsill and patio space make hanging baskets attractive to indoor and patio gardeners. They are especially nice when planted with trailing or cascading plants, and may contain several different compatible varieties.

Wire baskets should first be lined with sphagnum moss, then with a layer of black plastic punched with holes for drainage. Fill the basket halfway with potting mix, and set the plants in place. If you are mixing varieties, put an upright plant in the center and cascading ones on the edges. Fill the basket with soil, pressing firmly around the roots of the plants, and water thoroughly. Since these baskets are open to evaporation, they need watering more frequently.

Because of the water, these hanging baskets can become quite heavy, so be sure their supports are strong enough. Rotate the pot so that each side has its chance in the sun.

Herbs that are well suited for combination hanging baskets include thyme, prostrate winter savory, and rosemary. Nasturtium is lovely, but it is better planted alone because its mound of cascading foliage looks best when it fills a pot.

During periods of dryness, be sure to water your herb garden.

When digging plants from the garden to move indoors, you should first root prune them by running a spade down into the ground around the plant. Water the plant well and leave it in the garden for about a week so it can recover from the shock to its root system.

While it may seem brutal, there are further precautions that should be taken when bringing plants indoors. The first is complete repotting in sterile soil. Wash the plant's roots completely in a bucket of tepid water, having assembled all the supplies for repotting. Work the soil loose from the root crown with one hand, while supporting its stem and swishing the plant about in the water with the other. Wash the foliage in tepid water as well, checking under the leaves for any pests or eggs that might be clinging to the undersides.

Fill a newly scrubbed pot about one-third full with dry potting mix and tip it so the soil lies along one side. Lay the plant roots against this soil and fill the pot, shaking it slightly to firm the soil and being careful of the tiny root ends. An easy way to pack the soil snugly is to run a spatula blade down the edge of the pot and push the soil away from the edge with a prying motion. Then add more soil along the edge. Soak the soil thoroughly and set the pot in a shallow dish full of gravel so it can drain. If there has been considerable root damage, or if the plant is straggly at this point, prune it very conservatively to encourage more root and base growth.

All of this takes a little time, but saves you a lot of possible trouble later. Set the newly potted plant in a

Brightening this corner are various herbs, including rosemary and myrtle.

sunny window away from other plants for a week or so to give it time to acclimate, and to be sure it is not harboring pests that could start an epidemic. While it is not as essential to repot greenhouse-grown plants from a nursery, it is still a good idea, since, again, you could be bringing diseases or pests into your windowsill garden.

Containers are largely a matter of personal taste, but

they should be equipped either with drainage holes, or they should be large enough to make room for a good layer of coarse gravel or broken clay pot pieces in the bottom. While multiple containers—tubs or planters that hold several varieties—are attractive, it is difficult to find varieties of plants with the same soil and water requirements. It is better to use larger containers to grow several varieties of one herb, such as thyme. Individual containers are also easier to move about and work with.

Small pots and those without a layer of gravel in the bottom should be set on a tray of gravel or small rocks so excess water can drain. Also, as water evaporates from the stones, it provides moisture for the foliage.

Herbs such as tansy and tall achillea will survive winter without any attention from the gardener.

HYDROPONIC HERBS

It is quite fitting that herbs, which have found interest and use in each age of mankind's history, should move with the times. Hydroponics—growing plants in water—is seen by many as the hope for future food supplies, and if this is true, we need not worry about having plenty of herbs to flavor our salads of hydroponic lettuce.

Herbs respond beautifully to this method, succeeding where pot-grown plants have failed. You can purchase hydroponic planters with attached lights or you can make your own from two nesting plastic bowls and a desk lamp. The bowls should have flat bottoms; one of the bowls must be larger and at least two inches (seven centimeters) deeper so the smaller bowl can be suspended inside it with space at the bottom. Nesting bowls usually come in sets of four of graduated sizes and the largest and next to smallest usually provide the proper size difference. Punch holes about a quarter inch (.9 centimeters) in diameter in the bottom of the smaller bowl and push six-inch (twenty-one centimeter) strips of cotton bias tape through them so at least three inches of each piece extends through the bottom.

Fill the upper bowl to within an inch of the top with vermiculite. Mix up a quart of houseplant fertilizer as directed and soak the vermiculite well, letting it drain into the bottom bowl. When drained, the surface of the liquid should not touch the bottom of the upper bowl, but all the little strips of bias tape should reach it.

Insert small herb plants, their roots cleaned of soil, into the vermiculite, placing the plants close enough to touch. Place the bowl under a desk lamp fitted with a grow-light bulb, and keep it turned on twelve hours a day. Put this in a cool place and water with the fertilizer solution whenever the water level in the bottom pot drops and before the wicks dry out. Pour the water through from the top as you did in the beginning and be sure to check that it doesn't touch the bottom of the upper bowl. Herbs will grow quickly, providing plenty of fresh seasoning, even in this crowded environment.

Certain herbs do better indoors than others. Scented geraniums are used to being grown in pots, even outdoors, and make excellent houseplants. Bay and rosemary are not winter-hardy in many zones, and are frequently kept in pots outdoors and brought in for the winter. Marjoram, thyme, lemon verbena, pineapple sage, chives, lemon balm, winter savory, and miniature basils do well. A few of these, such as lemon verbena and chives, have special growing requirements that are discussed in "An Album of Herbs" (beginning on page 42).

Indoor herbs require regular watering, but should be allowed to drain well afterward, usually about twice a week. If they become too dry before that, they may need a larger pot or soil with a higher humus content. It is best to water indoor plants from below, standing the pots in tepid water until the soil is evenly moist, then allowing them to drain.

Narrow-leafed herbs, such as rosemary and savory, need a good misting with a sprayer every week or so, or set them in the bathroom when the shower fills it with steam. A dilute solution of fish emulsion is a good indoor plant fertilizer, necessary since the plants cannot send their roots deeper into the soil in search of nourishment as they would in the garden.

Patio gardens are a good place to use a variety of interesting containers. Large ceramic cache pots, wooden tubs, small barrels, iron kettles, terra-cotta pots, and long planter boxes all work well. These must have drainage holes or a good layer of gravel in the bottom for excess water. Position them so that each plant has at least half a day's sunlight and turn the

containers if possible so plants do not become lopsided trying to grow toward the sun. Water the plants regularly and remember that terra-cotta and other unglazed pottery act as a wick, allowing water to evaporate out of the sides of the pot. Like houseplants, these potted herbs should be fertilized occasionally.

You will find that potted herbs serve a useful pur-

Herb beds are so attractive that they are often used as ornamental gardens.

pose in your herb beds, too, since pots can be placed among the other plants to fill bare spaces until new plants are full-sized, and they can provide height to balance slow-growing plants early in the season.

Harvesting Herbs

Most herbs should be harvested as needed. Throughout their growing season, the snipping of a few sprigs or leaves for cooking keeps the plant trim and tidy. For larger harvests of herbs to preserve for winter use, the best time to pick them is just before the plant blooms, because the oils that give flavor and fragrance to the leaves are most concentrated then.

Perennial herbs grown in beds should be harvested so that the plants retain their shape, and so there is ample foliage left to support the plant. Annuals such as basil and summer savory can be harvested frequently by picking off the tops. This encourages the plants to grow bushier and send out side branches, as well as delaying their blossoming. Plants whose leaves grow from a central root crown, such as salad burnet, should be picked by cutting each stem close to the ground. This is also true of chives, which should not be cut across the top as if you were giving them a crew cut.

To keep harvested herbs fresh, put them in a vase of water or, in the case of parsley, chervil, and coriander, wrap them loosely in a damp paper towel and put them in a plastic bag in the refrigerator. Fresh herbs purchased at a farm stand or grocer's should be placed

The careful placement of plants allows even shaded areas to become lush herb gardens.

DRYING HERBS IN THE MICROWAVE OVEN

Since each oven has its own series of settings, you will have to experiment a little with your own. Fold fresh herb sprigs in a layer of paper towels and microwave on high for thirty seconds. Check the herbs and continue to microwave in thirty-second intervals until they begin to dry a little, then at fifteen-second intervals until they are crisp. Immediately seal the dried herbs in jars.

in water immediately, or stored in damp towels.

Gather herbs for drying early in the day, but after the dew has evaporated, and hang them upside down in loose bundles until they are thoroughly dry. The next day, hang the small bunches inside brown paper bags and suspend these in a dry, airy place until the herbs are crisp. The bags keep the leaves from dropping to the floor as they become brittle, and keep herbs free of dust and flies as well.

When harvesting blossoms such as yarrow, tansy, or costmary, which will be used in dried arrangements or for potpourri, cut them before the flowers are fully bloomed. They will continue to mature and ripen as they dry, and if they are full-blown when picked, they turn brown or fall apart by the time they begin to dry.

Preserving the Flavors of Herbs

Drying is the best way to preserve most culinary herbs, but a few need special methods. Basil, for example, turns brown very quickly when dried, and is better frozen. Parsley, too, is hard to dry successfully. Either of these may be frozen by stuffing the leaves tightly into plastic bags to form little bricks of herbs. They can be chopped directly from the frozen block by shaving with a sharp knife. Return the remainder to the freezer.

Herbal vinegars are very easy to make (see salad burnet, page 127) and can contain one herb or a blend. These are used in salads, marinades, and vinaigrettes,

© Rogers Assoc.

Herbal vinegars add flavor to salads, fish, poultry, and many other foods— and they brighten up the windowsill as well.

or any recipe where vinegar is called for. A splash of herb vinegar in the poaching water of eggs, for example, keeps the whites from spreading and imparts a delicate herbal flavor to the eggs.

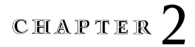CHAPTER 2

An Album of Herbs

Artemisia, Silver King and Silver Queen

Artemisia ludoviciana, **var.** *albula*

Artemisia's gray-green foliage and spikes of inconspicuous, matching, beadlike flowers are the mainstay of fresh herb wreaths, providing one of the best bases for other herbs. Of the two varieties, Silver Queen has wider leaves and fuller foliage, but the narrow-leafed Silver King provides better flower spikes.

Artemisia can easily grow to four feet (1.5 meters) in height and it spreads quickly. But a knowledge of its growth habits gives you the one trick you need to keep it contained. It sends out new underground roots only in the very early spring, when its gray shoots look as though they will take over at least an acre by July; but, there is no more underground spread until the next year. To prevent the shoots from spreading, draw a line with your trowel where you want the Artemisia to stop and pull all the shoots that appear over that boundary.

Artemisia is easily pulled or dug and its roots are quite sturdy, so this is the time to share it with friends or begin new beds yourself. Artemisia does require full sun, but performs well in ordinary or sandy soil.

ARTEMISIA, SILVER KING

The foliage can be harvested anytime, or after the beads have formed attractive spikes. Heavy frosts will change its color, but artemisia withstands light frosts easily. Strip off the blackened lower leaves if necessary and hang or stand stems in bundles if you choose to dry it for arrangements.

Named for Artemis, the Greek goddess of the moon and the hunt, the herb was believed to be possessed of her magical powers, protecting those who carried or used it from disease, fatigue, and the ravages of wild beasts. In this spirit, a wreath of artemisia on your door is a warm welcome to a safe haven!

Opposite page: Gardeners with a sloping area might grow herbs on a series of low-walled terraces cut with paths.

ARTEMISIA, SILVER QUEEN

An Artemisia Wreath

To make a wreath, wind fresh-picked artemisia around a single wire wreath frame while it is soft and supple, holding it in place with a fine, unenameled wire. Use plenty of stems, staggering them to make the base full and even.

After the base of the wreath has been formed, it may be hung to dry and decorated later; or, if you want to use it fresh, you can decorate it immediately. The base will need more sprigs of artemisia added to fill it out, but at this time use only the flowering spikes and upper leaves, pushing sprigs of these into the wreath in the same direction as the wrapped base. The wreath

The rich red of rose hips is the perfect contrast to the soft gray-green foliage of artemisia.

can be as full or as airy as you like, and other background herbs, such as horehound, sage, or rosettes of lamb's ears, may be added as well.

Once the background is filled to your taste, it is time to decorate the wreath with dried blossoms and seed heads. The pink-violet flowers of pot marjoram are a perfect contrast to the gray-green of the artemisia, as are the delicate pink blossoms of chive, lavender, bee balm seed heads, dark green bay leaves, and rosemary sprigs. Dried, fragrant rosebuds can be wired to florist picks in groups, as can tiny sprigs of dried flowers and herbs whose stems are too weak or too short to hold when pushed into the artemisia base. Costmary, tansy, and yarrow flowers all dry to golden yellow clusters that provide accent colors, as do any of the varieties of everlasting flowers, such as statice, strawflowers, acrolinium, Chinese Lantern, and baby's breath.

BASIL

Basil

Ocimum basilicum

No kitchen garden is complete without basil, and many gardeners who grow no other herb keep at least one basil plant. It is the one herb that the cook needs to have fresh. Its sharp, insistent flavor is the perfect foil for tomatoes, a discovery thought to have been made by accident when Italian cooks laid sprigs of basil over bowls of peeled tomatoes to keep flies away. However the flavorful affinity was discovered, basil is now considered essential to any tomato dish (and many other dishes as well), cooked or fresh.

Basil grows quickly from seed planted directly in the garden, but will develop into a larger, more foliant plant in northern zones if started indoors in flats.

Possibly the most frost sensitive of all herbs, it will

appear blackened in the morning after a touch of frost so faint that it spares pepper and tomato plants, so be sure it has early protection in the fall. Plants should be set at least a foot (forty-two centimeters) apart to allow for its bushy growth, and the growing tips should be pinched out when plants are about eight to ten inches (twenty-eight to thirty-five centimeters) tall to encourage branching. Flower stalks should also be removed, since the flavor and growth of the leaves both diminish when the plant blooms.

Along with the more common green basil, there is a striking purple variety attractive in garden and salad alike. Called Dark Opal Basil, it has the same flavor as common basil. For small gardens and windowsill plants, the compact bush basil is tidy and attractive, with the same characteristic flavor. Lemon basil has a distinct lemon flavor.

Basil does not air-dry easily, since its leaves quickly turn brown. The best way to preserve its color and flavor is to pack the leaves tightly into plastic bags,

Basil is the symbol of love, and a pot of basil on a lady's windowsill once signified that she would welcome a suitor. Today, a pot of it on the windowsill might attract suitors as well, since it shows that the occupant is a good cook!

Basil is the herb of choice with tomatoes, and both of them compliment the flavor of tortellini.

© Davies/Pashko/Envision

squeeze out as much air as possible, and freeze them. To use, unwrap the little frozen ball and cut off the needed amount with a paring knife.

In addition to its uses with tomatoes, basil is delicious with veal, chicken, and pasta, and is the primary ingredient of pesto (see recipe, page 50). This Italian sauce is used in a variety of dishes, most frequently in combination with pasta. Basil combines well with greens in salads but cannot sit once its leaves are cut; solve this problem by using whole leaves instead.

Basil Salad with Basil Dressing

6 peeled tomatoes, seeded
3 c. fresh basil, finely shredded
¾ c. olive oil
¼ c. fresh lemon juice
1 large clove of garlic
fresh ground pepper
½ lb. ham, julienned
½ lb. Fontina cheese, julienned
12 Greek olives, slivered
2 c. spinach leaves

To make the dressing, place half the tomatoes and half the basil in a blender with the oil, juice, garlic, and pepper and blend until smooth. Chop remaining tomatoes and mix in a salad bowl with remaining ingredients. Toss with dressing.

Serves 4.

Pesto is a versatile condiment and ingredient. It can be used as a filling or sauce for pasta, on raw tomatoes (here paired with mozzarella slices), or as a quick spread for garlic bread.

Basil Oil

Fill a jar loosely with sprigs of basil, taking care not to crush the leaves. Add pure olive oil to fill the jar. Seal and store in a warm place for at least two weeks. The leaves may be used in salads and the oil for any cooking use. The herbs and oil together are delicious stirred into hot fettuccine, and the oil can be brushed onto chicken while grilling. A clove or two of garlic may be added to the oil along with the basil, for a nice balance of flavors.

Basic Pesto

2 c. basil leaves, packed
4 cloves garlic, chopped
2 tbsp. pine nuts
½ c. olive oil
½ c. freshly grated parmesan cheese

In an electric blender, mix the basil leaves, garlic, pine nuts, and olive oil. Blend until fairly smooth. Add freshly grated parmesan cheese and blend just to mix thoroughly.

This should be stored tightly sealed in the refrigerator. If you plan on making a lot of pesto for freezing—a good idea if you have plenty of fresh basil—leave out both the garlic and pine nuts, adding them to the thawed pesto and blending together just before use.

Variations: Use almonds or walnuts instead of pine nuts. Make purple pesto with purple basil, or lemon pesto with lemon basil.

Use pesto as a sauce for hot pasta or toss a spoonful with freshly steamed vegetables such as zucchini, carrots, snap beans, or potatoes.

Herb vinegars, like this opal basil vinegar, make elegant gifts, especially when bottled in attractive glass jars with cork stoppers.

Thai Basil Chicken

This recipe is provided courtesy of Ronnerong Meng, chef and owner of the Chiang Mai Thai restaurant in Amherst, New Hampshire.

3 tbsp. fresh chili peppers, seeded and finely chopped
½ to ¾ c. basil leaves, coarsely chopped
2 tbsp. fish sauce, or white soy sauce (see note below)
1 tsp. sugar
1 tsp. rice vinegar
3 tbsp. vegetable oil
1 large onion in 1-inch pieces
1 large green pepper in 1-inch pieces
2 whole chicken breasts, boned, skinned, and cut in strips
2 cloves garlic, minced
½ tsp. cornstarch (optional)

Note: Fish sauce is a light-colored sauce used in Thai cooking as the Chinese use soy sauce. It has a delicate flavor, not at all like fish (the name refers to it being a sauce *for* fish). It is available at grocery stores selling Oriental foods. Dark soy sauce can be substituted, but the dish will lose the delicate color and flavor so characteristic of Thai food.

Mix chilies, basil, fish or soy sauce, sugar, and vinegar and set aside. Heat half of the oil and stir-fry the onion and pepper until just barely tender, but still crisp. Set vegetables aside and add remaining oil to the pan. Add chicken and garlic, stirring constantly until the chicken is cooked, about ten minutes. Return vegetables to the pan and add sauce mixture. Stir and cook until the sauce coats all ingredients.

If you prefer a slightly thickened sauce, add one-half teaspoon cornstarch to chili mixture in the first step.

Serves 4.

Basil Potatoes

⅓ c. olive oil
3 to 4 baking potatoes, peeled and sliced (approx. ¼-inch thick)
1 tsp. salt
freshly ground pepper
½ c. fresh basil

Line an edged baking sheet with heavy aluminum foil and drip a little oil on it, spreading it across the sheet. Arrange the slices of potato on the oil-covered foil. Pour the rest of the oil over them, coating evenly, and sprinkle with salt and pepper.

Broil the potatoes for about 12 minutes, making sure that they don't burn, but are a nice light brown. Turn over and broil approximately 12 more minutes. As soon as they are brown and crisp, sprinkle with basil and serve immediately.

Serves 4.

Wonderful tales had our father
of old—
Wonderful tales of the herbs and
the stars—
The sun was Lord of the
Marigold,
Basil and Rocket belonged
to Mars.

Rudyard Kipling

Bay

Laurus nobilis

One of the most elegant and lovely herbs in the garden, bay grows to a sizeable shrub. In northern zones it is usually set in a pot so it can be taken inside for the winter. It is a standby in the kitchen, yet few can describe its flavor, since it is not sprinkled over anything or used as a garnish. Rather, it lends its subtle flavor to soups, stews, and other long-simmered dishes. A bay leaf goes in the poaching water for chicken or fish and is always part of a bouquet garni.

Difficult to start from seed, bay plants are usually begun from cuttings. When purchasing plants, be sure to get culinary bay, sometimes called French, and not California bay, which has little flavor or fragrance. It will grow best in areas where it is spared harsh winter winds, since it retains its leaves year round.

On the island of Madeira, meat is broiled skewered on twigs of bay wood, which impart their fragrant flavor into the center of each piece. Two leaves placed just inside the skin on the breast of a roasting chicken will do the same thing.

The plant is a natural air freshener, and grows well indoors as long as it is kept evenly moist, so its roots neither dry out nor stand in water. Add a leaf of bay to containers of flour or other stored grains to keep weevils out of them. The flavor of bay will not affect the grain at all.

BAY

© Robert E. Lyons/PhotoNats

In the street market of Montparnasse in Paris, branches of bay leaves are sold singly or mixed with other herbs for a fresh *bouquet garni*.

A Bay Wreath

Only those who have an abundance of fresh bay can indulge in the luxury of a laurel wreath for their door or mantel, since it must be made while the leaves and branches are pliable.

To begin, use a crinkle wire frame and fine green florist's wire. Secure the end of the wire to the frame. Lay two or three bay branches, about eight to twelve inches (twenty-eight to forty-two centimeters) long, along the frame, their cut ends facing to the right. Wrap the wire around the lower four to six inches (fourteen to twenty-one centimeters) of the branches to hold them in place, but leave the top foliage sticking out. Working around the wreath toward the right, add more bay branches, each one covering the stems of the previous ones. Continue until the wreath is full and even. Move the branches around slightly, if necessary, to keep the shape tidy.

A few dried, bright red peppers can be added for color by attaching wire to their stems and tying them to the wreath, slipping the wire between the leaves to hide it. Garlic pods or shallots can be added, too.

If the wreath is hung indoors, it will keep its color. The wreath is a handy one for the kitchen, either fresh or after it has dried, because the leaves can be snipped off as needed.

Enter, solemnly tripping one after another, six personages clad in white robes, wearing on their heads garlands of Bays or Palms in their hands.

**Shakespeare,
from *Henry VIII***

A Bay Tree Topiary

Bay grown in a pot makes an attractive topiary and can be trained into a perfect sphere. Decide on the proportions you want so that the height of the finished ball will be a little less than the height of the stem; each (the ball and the stem) should be taller than the height of the container to create a well-proportioned plant.

The tree should be about six inches (twenty-one centimeters) taller than the height you plan for the finished topiary, and have a single, straight stem. Clip back the top (this will provide the rounded ball shape instead of becoming pointed) to the intended height of the top of the ball and prune off any branches below the bottom of the ball. Working inside the ball, prune back all the branches to the first set of leaves. Your tree will look terrible at this point, but pruning will cause each of those branches to form smaller, spreading branches. Once these grow you will need to cut each back to encourage even more bushiness, and the ball will be full, round, and well-shaped. All you need to do then is keep it trimmed of the leaves and tips that grow beyond your neat, round perimeter.

If the tree is in a window or a place where it doesn't get uniform light, turn it frequently to encourage even growth.

Fragrant bay grows wild in many seashore areas, such as this shore road at Cavendish on Canada's Prince Edward Island.

Provençal Bay Soup with Potato

10 c. veal or beef stock (chicken stock may be
*   substituted, but will not provide as distinctive a*
*   flavor)*
9 fresh bay leaves
5 large egg yolks, beaten but not frothy
Salt to taste

Simmer the bay leaves in the stock in a large saucepan for approximately 25 minutes. Remove the leaves. Cool 2 cups of the stock, then pour slowly into the eggs while mixing all the while. Pour the mixture back into the remaining broth slowly while still mixing. Heat the soup, being careful not to allow it to boil.

8 slices thick-cut French bread
3 to 4 tbsp. butter
2 large or 3 medium size potatoes
3 cloves garlic (more if you really like garlic)
Pinch of salt
⅓ c. fine olive oil
Freshly ground black pepper, to taste

Butter each slice of bread. Heat a skillet so that it will be hot enough to brown the bread, but not so hot that it burns the butter. Sauté the bread in the skillet until it is golden brown and set aside. Peel potatoes and boil until they are soft but not watery; about 20 minutes. Drain and press through a potato ricer. In a

The bay tree was sacred to Apollo, and his priestess at Delphi ate a bay leaf before delivering her prophesies. Bay was believed to protect against disease and witchcraft, and to the Romans it was a symbol of glory and honor. Heroes were crowned with the laurel leaf and even today we retain expressions such as "to rest on his laurels" and "Poet Laureate."

On Valentine's Day take two bay leaves sprinkled with rose water and lay them over your pillow when you go to bed at night. You will dream of your future spouse.

© Rogers Assoc.

blender or food processor purée the garlic with the salt. When it becomes a paste add the potatoes and mix until smooth. Slowly add the olive oil in a stream while beating to make a thick, smooth paste.

Ladle the soup into bowls and grind fresh pepper into the soup. Onto each slice of toast, spoon a generous serving of the potato mixture, then float the toast on the soup.

Serve immediately.

Serves 8.

Borage

Borago officinalis

From the days of the ancient Celts, who drank their wine with borage before entering battle, it has been associated with cheerfulness and courage. The classic herbalists all speak of borage's abilities to brighten and produce a sense of well-being.

One of the lesser known herbs, borage is also one of the most delightful rewards of gardening, since it is only used fresh. Its beautiful blue flowers are abundant and bloom continuously, so there are always some handy to float in summer drinks, garnish a salad, or chop into cottage cheese.

Borage grows quickly from seed and becomes quite large and sprawling, so be sure to give it plenty of room in your garden. In subsequent years new "volunteer" plants will spring up all around the previous one where the little black seeds have dropped. Since borage is hard to transplant, once it has reached any

BORAGE

significant size, it is best to move these volunteer plants while they are quite small. Plant borage between strawberry plants as they will improve fruit production.

The profusion of borage's blossoms and their neat star shape have made them a summertime favorite of children who string the flowers into necklaces. The leaves and flowers both have a cucumber flavor, making them a good addition to salads and drinks such as Pimm's cup #1. Be sure to use only the young leaves, before they get fuzzy. These may also be added to spring greens for cooking, and the blossoms contrast nicely when sprinkled on potato salad.

Borage Facial for Dry Skin

Put about a cup of young borage leaves in a blender with one tablespoon of spring water or rain water and blend until it forms a paste. Mix with a quarter cup of sour cream and apply to moistened skin. Lie down, propping your feet higher than your head, and place a moistened borage leaf over each eye. Rest for twenty minutes then wash the facial off with warm water.

Borage Cubes

Put a thin layer of water in an ice cube tray, filling it only about one-third, and freeze solid. Place one borage blossom, face down, in the center of each cube and add a drop or two of water. This will freeze the blossom to the ice. Carefully add just enough water to cover the blossom, but not enough to fill the tray.

Freeze again. Once frozen, fill the trays to capacity and freeze. Store these cubes in double plastic bags in the freezer for use in punch bowls during the winter holidays, when borage flowers are only a memory in the garden.

In Germany, fresh borage leaves are a favorite in salads. Here they are displayed in a Munich street market.

Add borage ice cubes to lemonade for a refreshing, and lovely, drink. Floating borage flowers on top will add to this effect.

Borage and Lemonade

1 lemon
1 tbsp. sugar
¼ c. boiling water
¼ c. cold water
2 ice cubes

Squeeze the lemon juice into a pitcher. Dissolve the sugar in a separate container of boiling water, and then add it and the cold water to the pitcher. Add ice, stir, and let set 10 minutes. Pour into a glass over ice and top with 4 to 5 borage blossoms floated face up.

CALENDULA (POT MARIGOLD)

Calendula

Calendula officinalis

When the poets sing of marigolds, it is of calendula, or pot marigold, that they sing. Calendula's history is a long and distinguished one, from its presence in Roman gardens to its medical use up to as recently as World War I.

Best known today as an ornamental annual, calendula adds color to food dishes and potpourri just as it does in the garden. Calendula is used in place of saffron to color rice (although it does not imitate saffron's flavor) and in puddings and salads, where it adds a pleasant tang. Calendula is a bright garnish for salads and sandwich trays, or add the petals to scrambled eggs.

Calendula grows quickly from seed and will bloom all summer long if faded blossoms are kept picked off. Northern gardeners will want to give it a head start by planting seeds in flats indoors, but in mild climates, calendula will bloom year round. The plants make a nice border, remaining tidy and compact, growing only between twelve and fifteen inches (forty-two and fifty-three centimeters) tall.

Calendula's cosmetic value made it a favorite in the

Elizabethan stillroom and it is still used for cleansing, softening and healing the skin. Preserving the fresh flowers in olive oil makes a beautiful addition to the dressing table and is a useful treatment for dry or chapped hands at bedtime. Or, soak hands in calendula tea made by pouring water over fresh blossoms.

When Constantine and his mother were searching for the True Cross she saw three crosses in a dream, with basil and marigold growing at the base of one of them. In remembrance, basil and marigolds are used in Eastern rite churches at the feast of the Elevation of the Cross.

Shakespeare mentions calendula as May buds, a name popular at that time, to describe morning when "winking May buds begin to ope their golden eyes." Keats wrote "Open fresh your starry folds / Ye ardent marigolds! / For Great Apollo bids / That in these days your praises should be sung / On many harps which he has lately strung."

Calendula is an herb useful in skin care and gives a splash of color to the herb garden.

Luxury for the Hands

3 tbsp. oatmeal
1 tsp. lemon juice
1 tsp. honey
Fresh petals from 3 calendula blossoms
1 tsp. glycerine

Whir oatmeal in a blender at high speed until it is almost powder. Pour oatmeal into a bowl; combine lemon juice, honey, and calendula petals in the blender. Mix until petals are well broken up and scrape mixture into the oatmeal. Add glycerine, and blend to make a smooth paste. Apply all over hands before bedtime and leave on for 20 minutes. (This is not the night for bedtime reading unless you have someone turn the pages for you!) Wash off in warm water, pat hands dry, and rub with a little olive oil in which calendula blossoms have been steeped.

Calendula Buns

1 c. flour
½ tsp. baking powder
¼ tsp. salt
⅓ c. butter
3 tbsp. sugar
¼ c. candied fruit peel
Petals from 2 large calendula flowers
⅓ c. milk
1 egg

Sift flour, baking powder, and salt. Break the butter up into the mixture and add the sugar. Mix in the candied fruit peel. Let the calendula soak in a muslin bag in the warmed milk. As the milk cools, add the egg and beat constantly so a smooth custard forms. Add this to the bun mixture and fold it in. Bake in greased muffin tins for 15 minutes at 350° F.

Makes 6 buns.

Calendula Pilaf

3 tbsp. olive oil
1 small onion, minced
½ c. white rice
½ c. orzo (rice-shaped pasta)
2 ½ c. hot chicken stock
Salt to taste
½ c. calendula petals

Heat oil in a heavy saucepan and stir in onions, rice, and orzo. Stir constantly to cook rice and orzo and to lightly cook the onions. When rice is opaque, add the stock and salt, stir well, cover, and turn heat to the lowest setting. When rice is tender but not mushy, add calendula petals and toss gently. Cover and leave with heat off for about 5 minutes to steam before serving.

Serves 4.

The Marigold which goes to bed with the sun And with him rises, weeping.

Shakespeare, from *Winter's Tale*

© Michael Grand

Calendula pilaf is a delicious, colorful addition to any meal.

Chamomile (Camomile)

Matricaria recutita and *Chamaemelum nobile*

We'll leave it to the botanists to sort out the differences between annual and perennial chamomiles, and to arrive at names and classifications for them. The herb gardener is of a more practical bent and is usually more interested in the fact that these two plants look, smell, and taste exactly alike.

CHAMOMILE

© Robert Perron/Sissinghurst Gardens

Taller and more erect in growth, *Matricaria*, known as German chamomile, is an annual, while *Chamaemelum*, or Roman chamomile, is low-growing and perennial. It is the latter which the English cultivate as lawns, but apart from that their uses are identical. Either one makes a luxurious and soothing bath herb as well as a softening rinse for blonde hair that brings out golden highlights.

Chamomile Shampoo

> 3 tbsp. fresh chamomile flowers
> 1 tbsp. fresh lavender flowers
> ½ c. boiling water
> 1 tbsp. liquid castile soap

Place the fresh flowers in a bowl and pour the water over them. Cover and let steep for a full day. Strain through a piece of cheesecloth. Add the soap and stir well. Pour in a bottle, seal well, and keep in the refrigerator when not using. When you do use it, rinse the shampoo thoroughly. This will keep for a week.

Chamomile Facial Cleanser

Steep three tablespoons of fresh chamomile flowers and leaves in a half cup of light cream in a double boiler for twenty minutes. Leave to cool, then strain and refrigerate. This is about a week's supply, which is as long as it should be kept. Pat on with cotton and tissue off gently.

Chamomile Tea

Chamomile tea is made from the blossoms, either fresh or dried, and is both soothing and relaxing, especially for those who have trouble sleeping; its sweet flavor is a favorite with children as well.

To make tea, steep 1 tablespoon of fresh blossoms in 1 cup of boiling water for 5 minutes and strain. For a delicious variation, include a few leaves of fresh apple mint (*Mentha suaveolens*).

Chamomile makes the perfect drink for afternoon tea.

Since the time of the Pharaohs, chamomile has been revered for its medicinal properties.

Chamomile reached literary prominence when Peter Rabbit drank a cup of chamomile tea after a particularly difficult day. Most gardeners would agree that it was Farmer MacGregor who deserved such pampering, not the pesky bunny!

© Michael Grand

Giant bundles of chamomile are brought from the Andean Highlands for sale in the weekly market in Gualaceo, Ecuador.

Though the Camomile the more it is trodden on the faster it grows, yet youth, the more it is wasted the sooner it wears.

Shakespeare, from *Henry IV*

Chamomile Lawn

While the moist climate of the British Isles is a far more suitable locale for growing a successful chamomile lawn than most, even in Britain it requires intensive labor and loving care. Few would choose to have a front lawn of it, no matter how sweet it smells when trod. But for a small area in an herb garden—perhaps just at the entrance, or between the paving stones of a garden path—a chamomile lawn is both fragrant and fitting.

When you buy your chamomile plants, be sure that you have the perennial variety (*C. nobile*). Set them four inches (fourteen centimeters) apart in a well-prepared bed free of weeds and stones. Water daily and weed by hand between the plants until they are well-established; when your chamomile lawn needs "mowing," trim it even with long-bladed paper scissors. Once the lawn is strong enough you can use a mower with the blade set high. Remove all flower heads as they appear and avoid walking on the lawn until it is well-established.

Chamomile Spray for Seedlings

Newly planted seeds in greenhouses and on windowsills frequently develop mildew since they must be kept moist at all times. Called "damping off," this eventually kills the little seedlings. This happens with moisture-loving houseplants as well. An effective spray to combat this mildew can be made by boiling a handful of fresh chamomile leaves and flowers for five minutes in two cups of water, allowing it to cool, and then spraying the strained "tea" on the plants.

Chervil

Anthriscus cerefolium

A subtle herb, often described as anise-flavored parsley, chervil is most often associated with French cooking. Since there is no way to preserve its flavor, it is the special province of the herb gardener who can snip it fresh. It blends best with fish, chicken, and salad vegetables.

Getting a chervil bed started may take a while, but once it is established it will self-sow for years. Sow the seed directly into the garden as soon as the soil can be worked in the spring and keep it watered until the plants are well rooted, which may be several weeks. Chervil does not transplant easily because of its long tap root. Plants run to seed quickly, so it is good to keep it manicured—not a problem for the cook.

Use chervil with fresh steamed vegetables, such as snap beans, carrots, and peas, but always add it at the last minute, since it turns bitter after long cooking. It is combined with parsley, thyme, and tarragon in a bouquet known as *fines herbes* in classic French cooking.

CHERVIL

© William Adams

Chervil is symbolic of new life or rebirth, possibly because its scent is somewhat reminiscent of myrrh. Because of this, chervil is often served on Holy Thursday in Central Europe.

Chervil Cheese Spread for Vegetables

6 oz. cream cheese
3 tbsp. chervil, minced
1 tbsp. chives, minced
¼ c. sour cream

© Jeanetta Ho

Chervil's delicate flavor blends well in this carrot soup, made from a chicken base.

Combine cream cheese with chervil, chives, and sour cream. Blend well to a spreadable consistency.

Spread on celery or carrot sticks, thick cucumber slices, or snow peas, or use as a stuffing for cherry tomatoes that have been hollowed out with a melon ball cutter. This mixture can be thinned with sour cream to a softer consistency and used as a dip for raw vegetables.

Carrot Soup

2 c. carrots, chopped
2 scallions, chopped
2 tbsp. butter
2 tbsp. flour
3 c. chicken broth
½ c. chervil, chopped
Grinding of nutmeg
Sour cream
Chervil leaves

Sauté carrots and scallions in butter until scallions are soft. Stir in flour and continue stirring until it is absorbed. Add chicken broth and stir until smooth. Simmer very gently, stirring often for about ½ hour. Purée in a blender until smooth. Return to pan and add chopped chervil and a grinding of nutmeg. Reheat and serve garnished with a dollop of sour cream and whole chervil leaves.

Serves 4.

Chive

Allium schoenoprasum

While these relatives of the onion are usually grown for the delicate flavor of their leaves, the blossoms will soon become a favorite seasoning for anyone who grows them. Unlike most other herbs, the foliage of the chive does not lose either flavor or productivity when the plant blooms.

Garlic chives (*Allium sativum*) have a flat leaf with a distinct garlic flavor—a boon to those who enjoy the flavor of garlic but cannot eat it. They can also be used to give a garlic flavor to salads and other uncooked dishes. They do not spread in the garden and may be

CHIVES

Chives form thick clumps that can be used as an edging in beds of taller plants.

planted closer together than other chives.

Chives are tidy enough to be used in the ornamental garden where their twelve-inch (forty-two centimeter) height makes them a good choice for a border or center planting. In the spring, when their deep green foliage is crowned with bright pink pompon blooms, they are as lovely as any plant in the flower garden. Although they can be started from seed, it is a slow way to begin a crop of something so useful. Purchase plants from a nursery or buy one of the pots in the grocery store and divide the clump at the roots to make three or four plants. Space these about twelve inches (forty-two centimeters) apart, since in a year or so they will fill in the space. Chives will self-sow if you leave the blossoms to mature, or they will multiply from the bulbs, but they are not weedy or hard to control.

© Frances Stein

Garlic chives are perfect for those who cannot eat garlic, because they provide the same taste without the "kick."

Growing Chives Indoors

Chives dug in the fall and brought indoors quickly become weak and straggly, a far cry from the robust plants they were in the garden. Even though they are in the house where it is warm, their inner clocks tell them that it is winter and time to be dormant. You can fool the plants into thinking that it is spring again if you plant them in pots and let them get established outdoors, then let them dry out a little, seal each pot in a paper bag, and store in your freezer. About six weeks before Christmas, take them out, trim off all of the dead leaves, water them well, and put them in a sunny window. Very soon, a healthy crop of new green shoots will appear and the pots will be full of chives, ready for use and in time for Christmas gifts.

Chive Butter

Soften ¼ pound of butter and add 1 tablespoon of chopped chive leaves. Mix well and chill 20 minutes. Spoon onto plastic wrap and shape into a long cylinder. Wrap again to keep out refrigerator flavors and freeze. To use, slice off rounds as needed for baked potatoes, hot breads, biscuits, or vegetables.

Chive Blossom Eggs

Mix 4 eggs with 1 teaspoon of milk and beat well. Pour into a buttered skillet and cook over low heat, stirring constantly. Just before serving, stir in the separated florettes from 2 to 3 chive blossoms.

By tricking chives into believing it is spring, it's possible to grow them indoors almost all year long.

Chives are a flavorful addition to hot pasta.

Chive Blossom Vinegar

Half fill a one-quart canning jar with fresh picked chive blossoms. Fill the jar with distilled white vinegar, seal, and place in a sunny window for two weeks until the vinegar is the color of rosé wine. Actually, the jar can be stored in the dark and do the same thing, but it is beautiful to watch the color deepen in the sunlight. The vinegar takes on a rich onion flavor perfect for salads, marinades, and vinaigrette.

Lemon-Herb Salad Dressing

1 scallion, finely chopped
1 tsp. Dijon mustard
3 tbsp. lemon juice
1 tbsp. dry white wine
1 egg yolk
1 tsp. garlic chive, minced
1 tbsp. parsley, minced
1 tbsp. chive blossoms, minced
Freshly ground pepper
¾ c. olive oil

Combine all ingredients except oil with a whisk, then slowly add the oil, beating continuously until completely blended. Season to taste, and chill before putting on salad.

Coriander is one of the rare herbs which, like dill and fennel, serve a dual purpose. Early in the season its leaves are used fresh; later, after seeds have formed and dried, they give a pungent, spicy flavor to baked goods.

Coriander (Cilantro)

Coriandrum sativum

One of the few herbs that produces two entirely different flavorings, coriander is best known in North America and Northern Europe for its aromatic seeds, which are used in baking and pickling. But in the Mediterranean, Latin America, China, and Africa, the leaf of this herb is a mainstay of local cuisines.

Coriander is easy to grow from seeds planted directly in the garden, but does not transplant well because of its long tap root. Check it often to remove flowering stems, since it will quickly go to seed in hot weather, at which time the leaves become spindly.

CORIANDER (CILANTRO)

"Long Standing," a new variety available from Vermont Bean Seed Company, resists going to seed and produces a crop of leaves over a much longer period.

Cilantro can be frozen in little bricks and shaved off like basil (see page 49), but cannot be preserved by drying. It does not keep long in the refrigerator either, so it is best to pick only as much as you need at one time. But, if you do refrigerate it, wrap it loosely in a damp paper towel and seal it in a plastic bag.

Unlike many herbs, there is no particular food that cilantro is associated with; rather, it is characteristic of several ethnic styles. Chinese, Mexican, and Italian dishes use it, as do several African and Near Eastern cuisines. The seeds are also frequently used in Moroccan and Scandinavian dishes.

Coriander was thought to have worked wonders in many ways during its long history: It was preserved in Egyptian tombs, the Chinese believed that it brought immortality, and in the Arabian Nights, it was used in a love potion.

Cilantro Dip

3 c. fresh cilantro leaves
1 c. scallions, sliced
4 fresh jalapeños, stemmed and halved
1 tbsp. salt
2½ c. sour cream

Place the cilantro, scallions, jalapeños, and salt in a blender or food processor, and blend until smooth. Add some sour cream if moisture is needed. When smooth, add the rest of the sour cream. Adjust seasoning, and refrigerate until serving.

Makes about 3 cups of dip.

Mexican Pesto

2 c. cilantro leaves
4 cloves garlic, chopped
2 tbsp. unsalted pepitas (special Mexican pumpkin seeds, available in most gourmet or specialty food stores)
½ c. olive oil

In an electric blender mix cilantro, garlic, pepitas, and olive oil. Blend until smooth. Store in refrigerator and use on pasta, chicken, or vegetables.

Cilantro Soup

2 lb. boned chicken breast meat, cut in strips
2 c. dry white wine
2 c. chicken broth
1 c. onion, minced
4 cloves garlic, minced
2 hot chili peppers, seeded and chopped
2 c. fresh cilantro leaves
½ c. fresh parsley leaves

Poach chicken in broth and wine until barely done (not over 10 minutes). Strain 1 cup of this liquid into a blender and add remaining ingredients. Blend until smooth; add remaining broth, reheat quickly, and add chicken. Garnish with cilantro leaves.

Serves 4.

Cilantro's flavor is unlike any other herb, but it is quickly lost in cooking. When used in hot dishes such as this soup, it should be added after cooking.

Cilantro is frequently used in Latin American cuisine, especially in the salsas of fresh vegetables that accompany so many dishes there.

Salsa

> 4 medium tomatoes, chopped
> 1 to 2 jalapeño peppers
> 2 cloves garlic, minced
> 1 medium onion, minced
> ⅓ c. fresh cilantro leaves

Place all ingredients in a blender and mix until smooth. Serve with chicken, tacos, or other Mexican dishes.

Makes 1½ cups of salsa.

Snow Pea Salad

> 4 tbsp. red wine vinegar
> 2 tsp. Dijon mustard
> ¼ c. olive oil
> 1 tsp. fresh ginger, minced
> 1 lb. snow peas, blanched and chilled
> 1 head red lettuce
> 1 red onion, thinly sliced
> 1 sweet red pepper, thinly sliced
> ½ c. fresh coriander leaves

Combine vinegar, mustard, olive oil, and ginger and mix well. Combine salad ingredients in a large bowl, add dressing, and toss lightly.

Serves 4 to 6.

DILL

Dill

Anethum graveolens

Like coriander, dill is grown both for its seeds and for its foliage; although they have very similar flavors, they are used in different ways. The seeds are a mainstay of pickling, where they are used fresh to make brined cucumbers. The same method can be used to make pickled green beans, snow peas, and onions. Dried, the seeds are used in pickling spice blends, along with coriander, clove, mustard, allspice, celery seed, bay leaves, and red peppers. The fresh leaves have a delicate flavor that goes with fish, chicken, and pork, as well as with vegetables.

There are three special varieties of dill with attractions for the home gardener. "Bouquet" is small and compact, more suitable for small gardens; "Nahne Herkules" is a German variety with elegant plumes of foliage; and "Dukat," from Denmark, has a large yield of both leaves and seeds.

Dill is easy to grow from seeds sprinkled on prepared soil, raked lightly. The surface should be kept evenly moist until the plants are established. Since the roots are very shallow, dill does not transplant well. For a continuing supply of both fresh seeds and leaves, plant at two-week intervals until midsummer. Leave a few heads to ripen in the garden to sow the next year's crop.

Whole dill heads that are ready to be pickled before the cucumbers are can be picked at their prime and stored in jars of cider vinegar. Rinse them off and they are ready to go into the pickle jars.

The best way to preserve delicate dill leaves is in olive or peanut oil. Pack the dill in the jar and cover it with oil. As it sits, the flavor permeates the oil, which can be used in salads and for cooking. Dill is a very versatile herb, but is most often used with potatoes, carrots, and salmon.

Dilled Cucumber Salad

1 c. walnut halves
5 medium cucumbers, peeled, seeded, and diced
4 c. plain yogurt
1 c. sour cream
⅓ c. fresh dill, minced
¼ tsp. salt
Dash of cayenne pepper

Toast the walnuts 15 minutes in a 250° F oven to crisp and enhance flavor. Cool and finely chop. Mix the cucumbers, yogurt, sour cream, dill, salt, and cayenne together well. Stir in the walnuts and serve.

Serves 6.

The flowers that bloom on the dill head are beautiful additions to any ornamental garden.

Dilled Chicken

1 c. plain yogurt
1 c. fresh dill, finely chopped
4 scallions, chopped (including the green end)
1 tbsp. fresh ginger, peeled and grated
2 tsp. ground cumin
2 green chilies, finely chopped
2 tbsp. lemon juice
Salt
Freshly ground black pepper
3½ lbs. chicken parts
3 tbsp. olive oil

Dill blends well with most seafood, but is especially at home with shrimp.

the chicken is cooked. Place the chicken back in the pan and add yogurt and dill mixture. Bring to a boil, cover, lower heat, and simmer for about 20 minutes, until the chicken is tender. Uncover, increase heat, and boil away most of the liquid, stirring from time to time. The sauce should be thick.

Serves 4.

Dilled Shrimp

1½ lbs. medium shrimp, in shells
1 c. dry white wine
3 cloves garlic
8 stems of dill with leaves
1 lemon, sliced
¼ c. red wine vinegar
2 tsp. sugar
1 jalapeño pepper, seeded and chopped
½ c. olive oil

Beat yogurt lightly with a fork until smooth. Stir in dill, scallions, ginger, cumin, chilies, lemon juice, salt, and pepper. Set aside. Skin the chicken, cutting breasts into 4 pieces, and everything else to pieces the same size. Salt and pepper both sides. Heat the oil over a medium-high flame. Put in one layer of chicken pieces, and cook to brown both sides. Repeat until all

Steam shrimp in wine with garlic until barely opaque. Drain and cool. Add 6 dill stems, the lemon end slices, and the remaining ingredients to the wine broth and simmer 10 minutes. While it simmers, shell the shrimp and lay them in a glass dish or jar with the leaves of the remaining dill and the remaining lemon slices. Pour the strained broth over the shrimp and chill overnight.

Serves 4 as a first course.

Vervain and Dill, Vervain and Dill Hinder witches from their will.

Dill's reputation for warding off witches caused people to wear little bags of it around their necks, while its ability to calm fussy babies led to making pillows of it for nurseries. Its name comes from the Norse "dilla," which means to lull.

Braised New Potatoes and Carrots

12 small new potatoes
12 baby carrots
1 tsp. salt
3 tbsp. butter
⅓ c. water
1 tbsp. fresh dill, chopped

Wash the potatoes and carrots and leave them whole. Place potatoes in a heavy saucepan with the salt, butter, and water. Cover tightly and cook for 20 minutes over low heat. Add carrots. Cover and cook for 15 minutes longer, or until carrots and potatoes are just tender. Add dill and mix lightly. Serve hot.

Serves 4.

A Dill Treat For Fingernails

Dill seeds contain silicic acid, a fingernail strengthener.

Mash four tablespoons of fresh dill seeds and pour one cup of boiling water over them. Allow to steep until cool. Soak nails for ten minutes, then pat dry. The mixture may be refrigerated for a second use.

There's fennel for you and columbines.

Shakespeare, from *Hamlet*

Fennel

Foeniculum vulgare

A close relative of the thick-stemmed vegetable Florence Fennel (*Foeniculum vulgare*, var. *dulce*), the herb fennel is taller and is grown for its feathery, anise-flavored leaves and seeds. In the garden it looks much like dill. A friend of dieters, fresh fennel leaves curb the appetite, as does tea made from its leaves. Like dill it is used with fish, where it offsets the strong flavors and lends seasoning as well.

Fennel is grown the same way as dill and will reseed a bed if a few heads are left to mature in the garden. Be careful not to plant it near coriander, since neither plant does well with the other as a neighbor. There is a bronze variety with elegant dark foliage, but its leaves don't look as good for food uses.

The leaves of fennel blend well with fruit—try a sprig of it in applesauce, and snip its leaves into a salad of sliced, peeled oranges and red onions. Fennel leaves mixed into melted butter make a delicious sauce for fish. Fennel leaves do not dry well, so should always be used fresh.

As a cosmetic herb it is just as useful. The seeds are a breath sweetener and the fresh leaves, used in a bath, are cleansing and lightly astringent. Buttermilk and fennel seed cooked together over a double boiler, then allowed to cool, make a deep cleansing lotion for oily skin.

Fennel gave the name "marathon" to the long distance run, for the battle of Marathon was fought in a field of fennel (the Greek word for which is *marathon*).

Even then its ability to curb the appetite was well-known. Fennel was thought to dispel witches (as well as fat), and bunches of it were hung over cottage doors for that purpose.

FENNEL

Fennel can be fairly untidy in its growth and is often put in the corner of a vegetable garden.

© Anita Sabarese

Hemingway's Scallop Mousse

The next two recipes are courtesy of Hemingway's, a French country inn in Killington, Vermont.

> *1 sprig of fresh fennel*
> *¼ c. olive oil*
> *2 medium shallots, finely chopped*
> *2 garlic cloves*
> *1 tsp. whole black peppercorns*
> *¼ c. sherry vinegar*
> *2 c. fish stock*
> *1 fresh sprig of thyme*
> *1 bay leaf*
> *1 tbsp. butter*
> *2 lbs. fresh sea scallops*
> *Salt to taste*
> *Pepper to taste*
> *Pinch of nutmeg*
> *⅓ c. dry vermouth*
> *Juice of half a lemon*
> *1 pt. heavy cream*

Combine fennel, oil, half of the shallots, garlic, peppercorns, vinegar, half of the fish stock, thyme, and bay leaf, in a pot. Bring to a boil. Reduce liquid by two thirds.

Place butter in a saucepan and heat until bubbling. Add scallops, salt, pepper, nutmeg, vermouth, lemon juice, and the rest of the shallots. Simmer 5 minutes.

Remove from heat. Pour the above reduction through a sieve into the scallop mixture, and then blend all of this to a smooth consistency in a food processor. To cool, place on a bed of ice, stirring occasionally.

In another bowl, whip the cream until stiff and fold evenly into the scallop mixture. Fill small ramekins to the top (or partially fill soup cups). Cover and refrigerate 4 hours. Remove from refrigerator and let sit a half hour before serving. Invert the ramekin onto a plate. Ladle the following Rosé sauce around the mousse and garnish with fresh fennel greens.

Serves 8 to 10 as a first course.

Rosé Butter Sauce

3 tbsp. rosé wine
3 tbsp. red wine vinegar
1 tbsp. minced shallots
1 c. chilled unsalted butter
⅛ tsp. minced saffron
Salt and freshly ground pepper

Combine wine, vinegar, and shallots in a saucepan over medium heat and reduce until mixture is syrupy and about 3 tablespoons of liquid remain. Remove from heat and immediately stir in 2 tablespoons of the

The Rosé Butter Sauce is a delicate accompaniment to white fish, as well as to scallop mousse.

butter with a whisk. Return to the heat and add the remaining butter, 2 tablespoons at a time, whisking thoroughly to incorporate butter. When ready, the sauce will be thick and creamy. Remove from heat and stir in saffron, salt, and pepper. Do not reheat or it will separate and become oily. Set pan over a bowl of warm water to keep warm. Ladle sauce around mousse.

Garlic

Allium sativum

Few flavors boast fiercer partisans than garlic. Almost universal in its use, it is the mainstay of Mediterranean cooking. It blends with all meats and most vegetables, and for many cooks a meal without garlic is almost unthinkable.

Garlic is very easy to grow. Simply separate one head of fresh garlic into cloves, and plant them in a pot pointed end up. (An old belief is that garlic will thrive if olive stones are planted next to each clove.) It is tempting to use the mild-flavored green shoots in salads, but if you do this too often it will weaken the bulb so that it won't multiply. Late in the summer these green shoots will die back, and a few weeks later the new pods can be dug. The best way to store garlic is by hanging it in an airy place. Traditionally, the tops

GARLIC

© William Adams

are braided into strings that can hang in the kitchen for easy access.

Along with *allium sativum*, there is the giant *allium tuberosum*, or "Elephant Garlic," not really garlic, but with the same characteristics. A typical clove is eight times the size of regular garlic and its flavor is a bit milder.

Garlic takes on a bitter flavor when frozen, so it is best left out of dishes headed for the freezer. It can be added before serving. Fed to your dog, it will keep fleas away (and it may keep you away, too). Its aftertaste is usually controlled by including parsley in any dish containing garlic. (Chewing a sprig of fresh parsley will cleanse the breath as well.)

Legend and science sometimes come full circle. According to legend, garlic is a deterrent to vampires. Recent research into a rare disease that has a number of symptoms which would explain the strange, vampirelike behavior of some individuals, shows that the disease is aggravated by a substance found in garlic. You've already guessed the rest of the story: Count Dracula is known to have suffered from the disease.

© Nancy Hill

Garlic, a mainstay of Mediterranean cooking, is sold in street markets by the string or bunch. Here, it is piled high in a market in Nice, France.

Eggplant and garlic have a culinary affinity so strong that one rarely finds a recipe for eggplant that does not contain garlic.

Garlic-Baked Eggplant

Slice several cloves of garlic and roll in a mixture of 1 part salt to 2 parts minced basil. With the tip of a knife, make slits about 1 inch (35 centimeters) apart all over the surface of an eggplant and push a seasoned garlic slice into each slit. Drizzle with olive oil and bake at 350°F until the eggplant is soft, about 30 to 45 minutes. This dish, from Provence, is delicious with lamb.

Lamb Patties

6 garlic cloves
2 tbsp. parsley, minced
½ c. dry bread crumbs
2 tbsp. olive oil
12 lamb patties

Chop garlic and mix with parsley, bread crumbs, and olive oil. Make twelve very thin lamb patties of ground lamb. Divide the garlic mixture between six of these, making a small mound on the center of each. Top each patty with one of the remaining patties and seal the edges. Press together gently. Grill or broil until done and serve on a toast round.

Makes 6 patties.

Garlic Chicken

10 to 12 garlic cloves
Roasting chicken
1 carrot, sliced
1 celery stalk
1 small onion, peeled
1 piece of bacon, uncooked

Peel the garlic and tuck the cloves between the skin and meat of a roasting chicken wherever the skin can be separated without tearing. Put any remaining garlic cloves in the cavity, along with a scraped carrot, a stalk of celery, and a small, peeled onion. Do not close the cavity. Rub the skin with a piece of bacon, and leave it draped across the breast. Bake at 375°F until the leg joint moves easily and the juices run clear.

Garlic enhances the mild flavor of poultry without overpowering it, even when large quantities are used.

© Frances Stein

GINGER (''BUTTERFLY GINGER'')

Ginger

Zingiber officinalis

Ginger is indigenous to the Orient, and was imported to Europe over 4,000 years ago. The first gingerbread boy may have been eaten in ancient Greece, where the art of baking with this flavorful rhizome was well-known. Commonly used in its dry, powdered form, ginger is far more versatile when used fresh.

Although it is only hardy from zone nine southward, ginger can be grown as an attractive houseplant. The easiest way to start a plant is to buy a piece of firm, fresh, gingerroot from the grocer and plant it in a large pot. It will sprout and grow into a sword-leafed plant that does not require full sun. As long as it can be kept evenly watered, it can live outdoors in its pot during the summer. Don't expect to grow enough for regular culinary use, but it is an attractive houseplant.

The sharp, spicy flavor of ginger goes well with meat and fruit. Slivers of candied ginger are a nice addition to fresh peaches and strawberries, and ginger is almost a necessity in peach preserves. Chutneys and curries contain ginger, as do many Chinese sauces and nearly all stir-fry dishes.

Medicinally, ginger has recently been found to be an

effective preventative for motion sickness, so some travelers carry candied ginger or ginger pills with them. Fresh ginger grated into tea relieves cold symptoms.

To store fresh ginger, bury it in moist sand, or slice it and put it in a jar of sherry. When the ginger is used up, the sherry is a delicious addition to stir-fry dishes. Fresh ginger should be sliced or minced and stirred in hot oil for dishes such as curry, but can be added without sautéeing to preserves and chutneys.

Gingered Couscous

2 c. couscous cooked with 1 cinnamon stick and
  2 bay leaves
3 tbsp. olive oil
½ c. onion, minced
3 garlic cloves, minced
¼ c. fresh ginger, peeled and minced
1 tsp. salt
Freshly ground black pepper
¼ c. pistachio nuts, chopped
½ c. fresh parsley

Discard the cinnamon and bay leaf from the cooked couscous. Sauté the onion, garlic, and ginger in the oil until the onion is translucent, about 2 to 3 minutes. Fold into the couscous with the remaining ingredients, and serve warm or at room temperature.

Serves 6 to 8 as a side dish.

© Jeanetta Ho

Couscous, a staple grain dish of North Africa, can be delicately seasoned with ginger as it cooks.

Ginger root is sold in the open markets of Munich, Germany.

Dost thou think, because thou art virtuous, there shall be no more cakes and ale? Yes, by Saint Anne; and ginger shall be hot i' the mouth too.

Shakespeare,
from *Twelfth Night*

Ginger-Peach Chutney

¼ c. whole mustard seed
4 qt. fresh peaches, peeled and chopped
1 c. raisins
1 c. onion, chopped
2½ c. brown sugar (packed)
5 c. cider vinegar
¼ c. fresh ginger, minced
1 small hot pepper, chopped

Toast mustard seeds lightly in a small frying pan, but be careful to keep them moving so they don't burn. Combine all ingredients and bring slowly to a boil, stirring until sugar is dissolved. Simmer until thick, stirring often, about 1 hour. Pour into hot sterilized jars and seal. Process 19 minutes in boiling water. Serve with curries, stirring a spoonful into the curry sauce when preparing.

Makes 8 to 10 jars of chutney.

Gingered Snow Peas

2 tsp. fresh ginger, minced
1 clove garlic, minced
3 tbsp. olive oil
2 sweet red peppers, sliced
1 lb. snow peas

In a wok, quickly sauté the garlic and ginger in oil. Add peppers and stir-fry until they are well heated, but still crisp. Remove peppers, ginger, and garlic and set aside. Add snow peas and stir-fry until barely tender. Return the pepper-ginger mixture to the wok and stir to reheat. Serve immediately.

Serves 4.

Ginger is a common ingredient in Chinese cooking and is the perfect seasoning for stir-fried snowpeas.

Horseradish

Armoracia rusticana

Until after the Middle Ages, only the Germans and the Danes welcomed horseradish at the table; to everyone else it was a medicine. As late as the seventeenth century an English herbalist noted that horseradish was eaten only by country people, it being too strong for the genteel stomach. Its acceptance finally spread, and today it is a popular condiment with smoked meats and beef.

Horseradish thrives even in poor, dry soil and will

HORSERADISH

spread underground. This habit, as well as its coarse appearance, makes it a good herb to plant in some far corner of the garden where it will not be destroyed by plowing, and where it can run wild. It is propagated from root cuttings or even from pieces of healthy fresh root, which can be purchased from the grocer. Buy a piece about eight inches (twenty-eight centimeters) long, and remove any side roots before planting. Well-worked soil without stones will produce straighter roots. Leave at least twelve inches (forty-two centimeters) between plants.

Roots can be dug late in the fall, but the flavor is best when the plant's strength is concentrated in its roots, just as it comes up in early spring. It can be stored, without loss of its ample vitamin C, in the refrigerator, but be sure to scrub it well first. It loses strength after grinding, so it is best prepared a few jars at a time. The best way to grate it, unless you have a head cold that you want to loosen up, is to peel (wear rubber gloves) and cut it in thin slices, and put it in a blender with a little white vinegar. Do not uncover it for a half hour; if it hasn't eaten through the glass container by then, transfer it to half-pint canning jars, top off with white vinegar, cover, and store in the

Huge horseradish roots are displayed in the open market in Munich, Germany, where they are ground and served with sausage and pork.

refrigerator. An interesting variation is to add a few fennel seeds to ground horseradish before sealing.

It can be used as is, mixed with mustard, or made into a milder, delicious sauce by mixing with equal parts of sour cream. This is especially good on beef and smoked tongue. The oil from this herb loses its flavor when exposed to heat, so horseradish adds no flavor to cooked dishes. When used in making prepared mustards, it is added after cooking. A slice of the root added to a jar of pickles before sealing keeps then crisp.

Chesapeake Bloody Mary

This recipe is shared by Scott Nock, chef of the Kent Manor Inn on Kent Island, near Annapolis, Maryland.

> *6 c. tomato juice*
> *2 c. clam broth*
> *3 tbsp. lemon juice*
> *1 tsp. celery salt*
> *½ tsp. black pepper*
> *3 tbsp. prepared horseradish*
> *Dash of Worcestershire sauce*
> *Dash of hot pepper sauce*

Combine all ingredients. Put 1½ jiggers of vodka in each glass with ice cubes and fill with tomato mixture. Garnish with celery.

Makes 4 tall glasses.

Horseradish Jelly

> *½ c. prepared horseradish*
> *7 c. sugar*
> *½ c. white vinegar*
> *½ c. liquid pectin*

Mix horseradish, sugar, and vinegar in a large pan over medium heat and stir until sugar is dissolved. Boil and add liquid pectin. Bring to a full rolling boil and cook 1 minute, stirring constantly. Remove from the heat to let foam settle for a moment, skimming only if necessary. Pour into jars, seal, and process 5 minutes in a boiling water bath.

Makes 5 jars of jelly.

A touch of horseradish adds zest to a Bloody Mary. Here, curly parsley replaces the more usual stalk of celery as a garnish.

Lamb's Ears

Stachys byzantina, syn. *Stachys lanata*

Leaves, stalks, and even flower stems of lamb's ears are covered with soft, fine hairs set so close together that they give the look and feel of velvet. This is a "comfort" plant that every gardener needs just for the pleasure of patting its leaves. Its magenta flowers grow on twelve to twenty inch (forty-two to seventy-centimeter) spikes that rise out of a mat of low-growing foilage.

Lamb's ears can be started by plant division or by seeds planted early in March. The plants can be set out as soon as they appear strong enough—leaves should be at least two inches (seven centimeters) long and rosettes should have formed. Allow about twelve

LAMB'S EARS

© Anita Sabarese

inches (forty-two centimeters) between plants for their spread. They are not invasive, but will fill a section of the herb garden or border within two or three years. They are a very attractive ground cover or edging plant and do quite nicely in partial shade. Although they thrive in all soil types, the richer the soil, the larger and fuller the leaves will be.

Leaves should be picked in clusters while they are soft, and dried face down on screens (for picks) and suspended through a screen (for stems).

The leaves and stalks hold their color and texture well, but the magenta flowers fade, leaving only the velvety stalk, which is well-suited to large, dramatic arrangements. The rosettes of leaves are beautiful on herb wreaths, especially with the pink blossoms of pot marjoram.

A Nosegay of Lamb's Ears

Pick evenly shaped rosettes of lamb's ears and fresh pink roses or clove pinks. Combine two rosettes to make an even ring of soft leaves. Group the roses or pinks loosely, and secure the stems with a wrap of wire or florist tape (always stretch this tape gently as you wrap to activate the adhesive). Slip the stems between two leaves so the flower bunch will sit right in the center of the circle of lamb's ears. Wire the nosegay together. Wrap the stems in a piece of damp paper towel, then in plastic wrap. Cover this with florist tape and, if desired, tie with a bow of dusty pink satin ribbon, leaving long streamers.

© Robert Perron

The large, soft leaves and pale color of lamb's ears set off other shades and textures in the herb garden.

Lavender

Lavandula angustifolia, also *L. officinalis, L. spica*

Lavender is the quintessential Victorian fragrance. Its scent filled the Victorian garden, parlor, and boudoir: Linens were stacked with sachets of its flowers in between and ladies refreshed themselves in the summer heat with fans woven of fresh stems.

In the garden, lavender is a compact and shrubby

In the Victorian language of flowers, lavender signified true love. Even earlier, Gerard suggested in his *Herbal* that lavender was "for the panting and the passion of the heart."

LAVENDER

© Rogers Assoc.

plant that can grow to a sizeable clump in zones where winters are not too severe. It is best started from root division, since plants started from seed may take two years to bear flowers. In mild, humid regions lavender makes a good, tall border. A bank of it planted near the clothesline will leave drying sheets fragrant with its scent. Flower spikes were traditionally laid or hung in linen closets to keep linens smelling fresh and clean during storage.

Lavender is perhaps best known for its cosmetic virtues and for heady-scented fine English soaps and lotions. Its name comes from the Latin verb "to wash," and at least since Roman times it has been associated with bathing. Later, its powers to invigorate and revive were used by ladies who carried vials or wands of it to sniff when they felt faint. A sprig of its blossoms in a footbath quickly revives tired feet, and several sprigs in the bathtub will invigorate the entire body.

Lavender Wands

One of the few crafts that must be done with fresh plants, lavender wands were a favorite of Victorian ladies, who made and carried them to alleviate fainting spells or headaches. Each wand requires an uneven number of long stems of freshly picked lavender flowers. The blossoms should be just barely open. You will need between nine and thirteen stems.

Tie these together just below the blossoms with very narrow (one-eighth inch [one-half centimeter]) satin ribbon in blue or lavender. You should allow

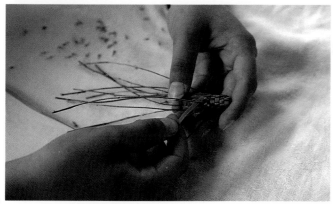

1. Stalks of lavender flowers must be fresh-picked for making into wands, so that the stems are pliable enough to be bent back over the bundled flowers.

2. Begin weaving the ribbon between the stems from the very top. It should be woven tight enough to hold the tiny blossoms inside as they dry and fall from their stems.

3. Continue weaving until the stems can be drawn close together below the bunch. Finish with a final wrap and a bow.

4. The finished lavender wand may be left to dry or used immediately to scent linen closets or bureau drawers.

about a yard (one meter) of ribbon for each wand.

After the stems are tied together, carefully bend the bare ends outward and over the cluster of flowers and weave the long end of the ribbon between them in a spiral. Leaving room for the flowers inside, weave the ribbon in and out between the stems forming an elliptical basket covering the blossoms. Tighten the weaving when you reach the end of the flowers so all of them are enclosed. At this point, tie the ribbon firmly around the bundle of stems and secure with a drop of glue.

Cut the ribbon and cover the knot with a bow made

Here's flowers for you,
Hot Lavender, sweet Mints,
Savory, Marjoram.

Shakespeare,
from *Winter's Tale*

from the remaining ribbon, leaving the ends long or cutting them, as you wish. Trim the ends of the stems even at the bottom.

The flowers will dry inside and be caught in the basket as they fall from the stems. The wands remain fragrant for years.

Lavender Bath

Make a bouquet of two spikes of lavender flowers and one each of peppermint and borage, tying them together. Float this in a tub of warm water.

A lavender bath is invigorating and slightly astringent. It is best for normal or oily skin types.

Lavender Hair Rinse

Lavender makes a good hair rinse to brighten gray hair: simply steep a handful of flowers in a pint of boiling water. When it cools, strain it and use as a final rinse water after shampooing.

Lavender Cosmetic Vinegar

Cosmetic vinegars may be diluted and used as a hair rinse. The vinegar restores the acid mantle to hair as well as neutralizing any shampoo residue.

Courtesy Gardener's Eden

The smell of lavender freshens any room. When placed in bunches in a wicker basket, it also enlivens any room.

Bring one cup of distilled white vinegar to a boil and pour it over a half cup of fresh lavender flowers. Cover and leave for twenty-four hours before straining and bottling.

For a skin-softening and restoring bath, add a half cup to a tub of warm water. To use as an astringent lotion for oily skin, add one tablespoon of the vinegar to a half cup of rainwater and splash on face. For a luxurious face wash, mix one tablespoon of the vinegar into a half cup rosewater. As a hair rinse, add two tablespoons of vinegar to a pint of rainwater.

Lavender Ice Cream

½ c. honey
1 sprig fresh lavender, blossom end
1 c. half-and-half
2 c. whipping cream
4 egg yolks

Warm honey and lavender in a stainless steel saucepan for 5 minutes, until the honey is flavored to your taste. Heat the half-and-half and the whipping cream in a saucepan, and whisk the yolks in a bowl until just broken up. Whisk a little hot cream into the yolks and return the mixture to the pan. Cook on low heat, stirring constantly, until the mixture coats a spoon. Mix in honey and chill. Freeze according to the instructions of your ice cream freezer.

Makes 1½ pints of ice cream.

Lavender ice cream is the perfect intermezzo for a meal with several highly seasoned courses.

leaves fill a cup of hot tea with their intoxicating flavor.

Balm is easy to grow, a perennial that can be started from seeds, nursery plants, or root cuttings. It spreads to tidy clumps, but does not invade with wild abandon like its cousin, mint. It is one of the few herbs that grows well in partial shade.

When the leaves are dried they lose their lemon fragrance, so they must be used fresh. Their texture is a little tough, so if they are used in a fruit compote they should be chopped very fine. In any dish that requires cooking, the balm should be added at the last minute, so that the flavor has just the right amount of time to permeate without losing its volatile oils. In cooking it does best in dishes where its steam can penetrate the surrounding food.

Lemon balm has a special household use that alone

Lemon Balm

Melissa officinalis

There is no herb so cheering to the weary gardener on a warm day as lemon balm. To simply reach down and pat its leaves, thus releasing its heady lemon fragrance into the summer air, is a reward well worth the work of gardening. The temptation to pick a sprig and put it into a tall glass of iced lemonade, a delight to the nose as you drink, is irresistible. And on a chilly fall day when the lemon balm is still green in the garden, its

LEMON BALM

Iced tea with a sprig of lemon balm is a refreshing summertime drink.

would make it worthy of garden space. Its leaves, rubbed on furniture, give a lustrous shine to the wood—it is the oil used in lemon oil furniture polish. As a bonus, cats will avoid furniture rubbed with lemon balm.

Lemon Balm Vinegar

Pack lemon balm leaves into a jar until it is half filled. Fill the jar with distilled white vinegar and set aside for two weeks to steep. Use in salads or sprinkle over cucumber slices.

Lemon Risotto

1 c. short grain (arborio) rice
2 tbsp. olive oil
2 tbsp. onion, minced
1½ to 2 c. chicken broth
2 sprigs lemon balm

Sauté rice in olive oil with onion. When rice is opaque, add 1 cup of boiling chicken broth and cook over lowest heat, uncovered, until the broth is absorbed. Add another ½ cup of broth and stir gently. Remove from heat, bury the sprigs of lemon balm in the rice and cover the pan. Let steam 5 minutes and serve garnished with lemon balm leaves.

Serves 4 as a side dish.

Lemon Wine Bowl

1 c. lemon balm leaves
2 qt. boiling water
1 c. sugar
¾ c. freshly squeezed lemon juice
2 bottles white wine (Rhine and Mosel are best)

Steep lemon balm leaves in boiling water, stir in sugar, and allow to cool. Add lemon juice and white wine, and chill. To serve, pour into a punch bowl over ice cubes in which individual lemon balm leaves have been frozen (see borage, page 57). Garnish with lemon balm sprigs in each glass.

Makes 16 glasses.

© Judd Pilossof

Known as the elixir and restorer of life, lemon balm has been credited with the long lives of a number of people who drank lemon balm tea each day. History doesn't mention whether or not the tea was mixed with white wine!

The light flavor of lemon balm is a natural seasoning for Italian risotto. This one is dressed up a bit with a garnish of capers, but it could also have a sprig of lemon balm at its center.

A plain canning jar is perfect for making sun tea. Lemon balm leaves give it a piquant lemon flavor.

As sweet as Balm, as soft as air, as gently.

**Shakespeare,
from *Antony and Cleopatra***

Lemon Sun Tea

On a hot sunny day, put 1 tablespoon of loose tea leaves and 3 to 4 sprigs of lemon balm in a quart jar. Fill with cold water, cover, and set in the sun. When the water has become a rich amber color, put the jar in the refrigerator to cool, then strain over ice and garnish with fresh lemon balm leaves.

Makes 4 glasses of tea.

Lemon Balm Jelly

> *1 c. fresh lemon balm*
> *2¼ c. water*
> *2 tbsp. fresh lemon juice*
> *3½ c. sugar*
> *½ bottle liquid pectin*
> *1 drop green food color*

Boil the water with the lemon balm in it, then let cool for 10 minutes. Strain. Measure out 1¾ cups of the mixture and mix that with the sugar and lemon juice. Bring to a boil, then add the pectin and coloring. Boil while stirring constantly for 1 minute. Skim off the foam as soon as you have taken it from the heat and pour into sterilized jelly jars. Seal jars and process 5 minutes in boiling water.

Serve on delicately flavored tea breads or scones.

Makes approximately 5 jars of jelly.

Marjoram and Oregano

Origanum majorana, Origanum hirtum,
Origanum vulgare

So confusing are the botanical classifications for this family that the gardener is better off relying on a good sense of taste than on the arguments of botanists. No two nurseries or seed houses agree on names. What one calls wild oregano another calls pot marjoram. Since there is no telling what will come up from seeds in this family (it is most often the tasteless pot marjoram) it is safer to buy nursery plants which give off a distinctive scent when rubbed (or flavor when nibbled). Marjoram has a milder, sweeter, but very noticeable scent, while oregano is stronger and sharper. But each plant varies greatly in taste, so the best way to be sure that you like one is to taste it. Since uses for the two herbs are similar, the fact that one blends into the other almost imperceptibly is not a problem.

Varieties such as golden marjoram are easier to recognize because of their bright yellow leaves. Its flavor is mild and savory, less pungent than oregano. Pot marjoram has almost no flavor at all, but its deep pink flowers are among the most beautiful for dried flower arrangements. These are rarely grown commercially, despite their long-lasting magenta color and the ease with which they dry when stood in a dry vase.

All of the varieties of these two herbs are very easy to grow, although oregano is less hardy in northern climates, and pot marjoram the most hardy of all. All will spread to form clumps, but none is invasive. The culinary varieties are dried by hanging, and retain their flavors very well. Harvest just before they bloom for the strongest flavor, and propagate by making root divisions in the spring or fall. Both grow fairly easily indoors if plant tips are kept snipped off.

Both marjoram and oregano are used in Italian cooking and, while the dried herbs work well in sauces and cooked dishes, there is no substitute for fresh marjoram leaves to brighten a salad. Oregano adds a lusty tang to sliced tomatoes, and it is, of course, the favorite herb for pizza. Marjoram sprigs laid over and

MARJORAM (LEFT) AND OREGANO (RIGHT)

Tasting a leaf is the only sure way to determine the flavor of members of the oregano/marjoram family. These are often labelled in confusing ways by seed houses and nurseries.

under roasting meat, or rolled inside roasts, add a savory touch that is hard to define, but delicious.

Oregano tea makes a good hair conditioner for those who don't mind smelling a bit like pizza, and is also valued for a relaxing bath. Both herbs are used as air sweeteners, which gives double value to a bouquet inside the house.

No Italian "hero" is respectable without a sprinkling of fresh marjoram leaves, or at least a little dressing made with olive oil in which it has steeped. Oregano oil is made in the same way as basil oil (see page 49).

Scallops Oregano

1 lb. bay scallops
2 cloves garlic, finely minced
3 tbsp. olive oil
1 tbsp. fresh parsley
1 tbsp. fresh oregano
Pepper to taste

Sauté scallops and garlic in olive oil. When scallops are just white (they should not be overcooked), add parsley, oregano, and a few gratings of pepper. Stir gently and serve. Do not try to double this recipe in one pan. If you need to make more, cook simultaneously in two separate pans.

Serves 4 as a main course.

Grilled Lamb

1 leg of lamb, boned, and cut into 2-inch cubes
2 c. olive oil
1 c. dry red wine
6 cloves garlic, minced
¼ c. fresh oregano, chopped
2 to 3 sprigs rosemary
6 to 8 peppercorns
2 onions, sliced

Make a marinade of all ingredients but the lamb. Mix the lamb into the marinade and store overnight in the refrigerator in a covered bowl. Thread the meat loosely onto skewers and sear close to the coals for 5 minutes, turning once. Raise the heat of the grill and continue grilling until the meat is pink inside and tender.

Serves 6 to 8.

Indeed, sir, she was the sweet Marjoram of the Salad, or rather the Herb-of-grace.

Shakespeare, from *All's Well That Ends Well*

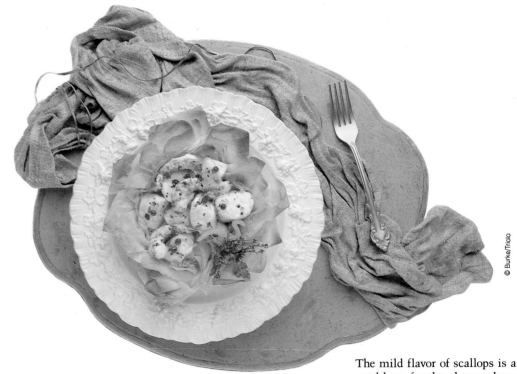

© Burke/Triolo

The mild flavor of scallops is a good base for the almost sharp taste of oregano.

Potato Salad

2 lb. small red potatoes
¼ c. plus 2 tbsp. red wine vinegar
¼ c. water
2 scallions, sliced
½ c. celery, diced
1 tbsp. fresh marjoram
2 tbsp. Dijon mustard
2 hard cooked eggs, sliced
20 Greek olives
4 tbsp. olive oil

Boil the potatoes in salted water until just tender, and drain. Cut the potatoes into chunks. Marinate potatoes in ¼ cup vinegar, water, and scallions for 1 hour, stirring often. Drain and add celery and marjoram. Mix oil, 2 tablespoons vinegar, and mustard and pour over salad. Garnish with egg slices and olives.

Serves 6.

Oregano Pesto

1¼ c. fresh oregano leaves
¼ c. fresh parsley
1 clove garlic
¼ c. walnut meat, chopped
¼ c. walnut oil
¼ c. parmesan cheese, grated

Marjoram was the favored herb of Venus, who gave it its fragrance with her delicate touch as she cultivated it. Newly wedded couples were crowned with it, and the ancient Greeks planted it on graves to ensure the deceased eternal happiness.

Mix oregano leaves (if you don't have enough use half oregano and half marjoram), fresh parsley, garlic, walnuts, and walnut oil in a blender until smooth. Add parmesan cheese and stir into hot fettuccine. This is a robust blend, so use it more sparingly than you would basil pesto.

Makes 1 cup of pesto.

Portuguese Skewered Meat

Lamb or beef cubes
Onions
Red pepper
Green pepper
Plum tomatoes
Stems of oregano or marjoram

This recipe is an example of some of the innovative ways in which the Portuguese use the herbs that cover their hillsides.

Alternate cubes of beef or lamb on skewers with quartered onions, red and green pepper chunks, and plum tomatoes halved crosswise. Grill close to the coals until the meat is the desired color. Remove quickly and carefully, and into each hole left by the skewers, push a single, small stem of marjoram or oregano. If you have these all cut and use a skewer tip to help them in, you can do this before the meat and vegetables cool. Use tongs to hold the meat.

SPEARMINT

APPLE MINT

PINEAPPLE MINT

Mints

Spearmint: *Mentha spicata*; Apple Mint: *Mentha suaveolens*; and Pineapple Mint: *Mentha suaveolens* var. *variegata*

Mints have a bad reputation among gardeners for their invasive habits, especially spearmint, which will take over an entire garden in a few years. Unlike artemisia, which can be controlled in the spring (see page 45), mint seems to send out its spreading roots at all seasons. These roots are deep, or will travel as deeply as necessary to escape their bounds. They will travel long distances, under a sidewalk or a stone wall if necessary, before popping to the surface. Even closely grown turf does not stop these persistent shoots.

The problem is not without solutions and the herb is well worth growing for its delicious flavor and aroma. The easiest solution is to plant mint in a metal tub—a galvanized washtub is perfect and makes a neat, round bed. A clay pot will eventually crack from the force of the roots, and any pot with a hole will allow one runner to escape, which will soon spread mint in every direction. Sink the tub in the ground almost up to the rim, but not below, or the mint will grow up over the edge. Keep it well watered during droughts and don't worry about drainage, since mint is one of

In Greek mythology, mint was the symbol of hospitality and was traditionally rubbed on a table to freshen it before it was set for guests.

The best way to keep invasive spearmint under control is to plant it in a metal tub or wooden box, submerged to the rim in the garden.

the rare herbs that can tolerate "wet feet."

The other solution is to plant the equally tasty, but less invasive apple mint—not quite as sharp a spearmint flavor, but with a pleasant, fruity undertone. Pineapple mint is very pretty in the garden with green and white variegated foliage. Its flavor is more pineapple than mint, a nice addition to iced summer drinks.

Mint is best known as a candy flavoring, but has culinary uses far beyond its usual association with sweets. Leaves of any mint are delicious in fresh fruit dishes, and go well with fresh cucumbers. The flavor of peas is enhanced when a few fresh mint leaves are added to the cooking water, and chopped mint leaves give the distinctive difference to Lebanese and Greek salads.

Popular throughout the Near East, mint is also used in Indian, Moroccan, Greek, and Arabic cuisine, especially in combination with lamb. Mint jelly or vinegar is often served with roast lamb and other fruit preserves served with meat often include it. Try making a pesto sauce (see basil, page 50) with mint leaves and cashew nuts and toss it with cooked bulgur wheat. Whole mint leaves frozen into ice cubes are an elegant addition to iced tea. Whole leaves can also be candied (see violets, page 139).

In the bath, a sprig of fresh mint leaves is refreshing and cooling in the summer, and a tea of spearmint is a soothing bath for chapped or rough hands.

Lebanese Tabbouleh

4 c. cooked bulgur wheat, cooled
1 c. chick-peas, cooked, rinsed, and cooled
1 c. cucumber, diced
1 c. thick flesh tomatoes, drained and chopped
½ c. scallions, finely chopped
½ c. Italian parsley, minced
½ c. spearmint, minced
½ c. olive oil
¼ c. fresh lemon juice

Combine all ingredients in a large bowl and chill well before serving

Serves 8.

Tabbouleh is a favorite food of the Middle East, and an excellent setting for mint, parsley, and other salad herbs.

Noisettes of Lamb with Fresh Mint

8 noisettes of lamb cut 1¼ inch thick, each
    wrapped with a strip of bacon around its
    diameter. (Your butcher will cut these from a
    boned loin or you can prepare them yourself.)
Bones and scraps remaining from the cutting of
    the noisettes
3 tbsp. olive oil
½ c. fresh mint leaves
1 medium carrot, chopped
1 onion, chopped
2 cloves garlic, pressed

1 bay leaf
1½ c. red Bordeaux wine
3 tbsp. chilled butter
Freshly ground black pepper

Trim as much lean meat from the bones as possible and reserve these scraps. Break bones into smaller pieces and simmer, covered, to make a rich lamb broth. Reserve 2 cups. Any remaining stock can be used in soup or for other dishes.

Heat 1 tablespoon of oil in a heavy skillet and stir in

© Brian Leatart

The flavor of lamb is enhanced by pairing it with the clean, fresh taste of mint. The two are traditional partners in locations as far apart as Greece and New England.

lamb scraps until well browned. Add 2 tablespoons of the mint leaves and the chopped carrot, onion, and garlic. Stir well while cooking to soften but not brown. Add the bay leaf and stir in the broth and the wine. Boil uncovered for 5 minutes. Lower heat and simmer, uncovered, for about an hour. Strain, pressing the juices from the solids and reserve the liquid.

Mince the remaining mint and cut the butter into small pieces. Sprinkle noisettes with pepper. Put 2 tablespoons of oil in a heavy skillet and, over a medium heat, sauté noisettes about 2 minutes on each side until medium rare. Transfer to a plate and cover with an inverted plate to keep warm. Increase the heat and add the reserved strained wine broth to the pan, scraping the bottom of the pan to deglaze. Bring to a boil, and reduce stock to 1 cup. Remove from heat and whisk in butter, 1 piece at a time. Stir in mint.

Remove the bacon and strings from the medallions. Spoon the sauce over the meat and serve.

Serves 4.

Frosted Mint Leaves

Choose perfect leaves of spearmint and wash them carefully, patting them dry with a paper towel. Beat an egg white lightly and, with a small brush, coat a leaf on both sides. Lay it in a saucer filled with superfine sugar and sprinkle sugar over the top to coat it. Turn the leaf and sprinkle sugar onto any spot where the sugar has not adhered. Gently shake off the excess and lay onto a rack to dry. Do not attempt to make these on a humid or cloudy day.

These are best made and used fresh, but they may be stored in sealed containers for a few weeks. Use to decorate cakes, tarts, fruit cups, scoops of sherbert, or serve them at teatime as elegant sweeteners for hot tea. They are delicious with lemon mint ice cream.

Lemon Mint Ice Cream

1 egg
2 c. whipping cream
1½ c. light cream
1 c. sugar
⅛ c. mint leaves, finely sliced
½ tbsp. lemon peel, finely grated
⅛ c. lemon juice
Lemon twists and fresh mint leaves for garnish

Beat the egg in a mixing bowl; when it is light, stir in the whipping cream, light cream, sugar, mint leaves, lemon peel, and lemon juice. Stir until the sugar dissolves completely and pour into the can of your home ice cream freezer. Freeze according to instructions.

Serve the ice cream in small sherbet dishes and garnish with the lemon twists and fresh mint leaves. It is a fine end to a summer meal and will brighten a hot day when served at teatime.

Makes 1 quart of ice cream.

Nasturtium

Tropaeolum majus

One of the brightest and most cheerful garden flowers, nasturtium has also earned its place in the herb garden. The leaves of the plant are peppery, but its tender blossoms moderate that piquancy with a floral overtone. Both the leaves and the flowers can be used fresh in salads, sandwiches, and as a seasoning for cooked vegetables.

In the garden they are most effective cascading over a stone wall or as a full border around large beds. If given enough space they will trail, making them a good choice for both hanging pots and window boxes. Seeds should be planted directly in the garden, since transplanting often causes stunted plants with long stems, tiny leaves, and no flowers. Soaking the seeds overnight can speed germination by as much as a week. Nasturtiums seem to thrive on salt spray, so they are a good choice for planting in seaside gardens.

NASTURTIUM

© William Adams

Mixed Salad

Red lettuce
Small, inner leaves of romaine
Bibb lettuce
Nasturtium leaves and flowers
Arugula
Parsley leaves
¼ c. olive oil
3 tbsp. lemon juice
1 tbsp. water
1 tbsp. chive leaves, finely chopped

Combine red lettuce, romaine, Bibb lettuce, small nasturtium leaves, arugula, and parsley leaves in a large crystal salad bowl. Add nasturtium flowers. Mix olive oil with lemon juice, water, and chives. Pour over salad and serve immediately.

Nasturtium Gelatin Salad

At their grandest in flamboyant summer salads against a bed of deep greens, nasturtiums are also elegant in jellied salads formed in ring molds. Pour a thin layer of lemon gelatin into a well-chilled mold; turn and tilt to cover all surfaces and place mold in freezer. Be sure it is level. When the gelatin is firm, pour in about a half-inch (two-centimeter) layer of gelatin, arrange perfect, fresh-picked nasturtiums face down inside the mold, making sure they are well

The vivid colors of nasturtium blossoms add a lively accent to the usual greens and grays of the herb garden.

anchored in the gelatin, and chill again in the freezer. Keep remaining gelatin soft by setting it in a bowl of hot water if necessary. When the chilled gelatin has set, pour in the remaining gelatin to fill the mold. If the nasturtiums are a very light color, make the last layer a dark red gelatin, black raspberry for example, to provide a contrasting background.

Nasturtium Vinegar

Half fill a canning jar with bright orange nasturtium flowers; fill with white distilled vinegar. Let stand for several weeks in a shaded place until the vinegar is richly colored. Use in salads of tender, mild-flavored greens.

Nasturtium Tea Sandwiches

Homemade bread
8 oz. cream cheese, softened
2 tbsp. sour cream
12 nasturtium blossoms, coarsely chopped

Remove crust from thinly sliced homemade bread. Combine cream cheese with sour cream and nasturtium blossoms. Spread thinly on the bread. Top with another slice of bread, cut in quarters, and refrigerate a half hour before serving to blend the flavors. Garnish plate with whole nasturtium blossoms.

© Michael Grand

Brilliant nasturtium blossoms and their neat round leaves make a perfect garnish for a plate of nasturtium tea sandwiches.

Chicken-Nasturtium Sandwiches

1 c. white meat chicken, diced
¼ c. cashews, chopped
¼ c. celery, chopped
2 tbsp. nasturtium leaves, finely shredded
2 tbsp. nasturtium flowers, finely shredded
Mayonnaise
Whole wheat bread, thinly sliced, crusts removed

Mix together chicken, cashews, celery, and nasturtium leaves and flowers. Add enough mayonnaise to hold the mixture together and spread on slices of bread. Top with another slice of bread and cut diagonally into quarters.

PARSLEY

Parsley

Petroselinum crispum

Probably the most common herb, parsley is the only one consistently available fresh in the supermarket. Its popularity, however, is often only as a garnish, a bit of green next to the fish. Parsley is worth more attention than it gets, both as a flavoring and as a partner for other herbs. Parsley blends and smooths the flavors of other herbs and neutralizes the after effects of garlic without dulling its flavor. For this reason it is very often used in combination with garlic.

In the garden it is slow to germinate and difficult to transplant because of its long tap-root. Legend holds that parsley must go to the devil and back nine times before the seeds sprout, and the impatient gardener can readily believe this. To speed germination and give the seeds a head start, freeze seeds inside ice cubes and plant the cubes. Not only does freezing help break down the hard coating, but the melting ice keeps the seeds moist as they begin to burst. Parsley is a biennial which goes quickly to seed in the second season, so it is best to plant it new each year. Leave second-year plants in the garden to provide an early crop until the new plants begin to produce.

Parsley doesn't dry well, but can be frozen like basil (see page 49). It can be dried in a frost-free refrigerator. by wrapping it loosely in a paper towel, putting that inside an unwaxed paper bag, and leaving it in the back of the refrigerator. In a few weeks it will be crisp-dry and still have its rich green color. Parsley's ability to take on other flavors can be used to clear deep frying oil that has been used for fish or seafood. After use, fry a few sprigs of parsley in the oil and the fish flavor will disappear.

Parsley Pressed Pasta

1½ c. semolina pasta flour
1 egg
1 egg white
1½ tbsp. olive oil
1 tsp. salt
1 bunch fresh Italian parsley, leaves removed from
  stems
Water

In a large bowl, make a well in the center of the semolina. Put egg, egg white, oil, and salt in the well and mix together with your fingers to form a rough ball. Collect the extra flour and crumbs with the water. Knead smooth, either by hand or in a food processor. Roll out as thin as possible, and lay the strip down on a work surface. Place parsley leaves on one end of the strip, close together. Fold the other end over them, and carefully run through the pasta machine on a couple of settings wider than the strip was last rolled on. Gradually work back to the thinnest setting. Cut the strip into 2-inch squares, and let dry on a cooling rack. Store in an airtight container.

Makes 1 pound of pasta.

ITALIAN PARSLEY

Garbanzo Parsley Salad

4 c. cooked garbanzos (chick-peas), drained and
  rinsed
1 c. cannelloni beans
3 Italian plum tomatoes, coarsely chopped
1 green pepper, chopped
1 sweet red pepper, chopped
4 scallions, chopped
½ c. whole parsley leaves, removed from stems
1 tbsp. fresh mint leaves, chopped
1 head Bibb lettuce
¼ c. olive oil
2 tbsp. balsamic vinegar
1 tbsp. water

Mix beans, vegetables, and parsley. Mix oil, vinegar, and water and combine with vegetables. Chill 1 hour. Line a plate with the Bibb lettuce and mound the salad in the center.

Serves 8.

Chimichurri

¼ c. red wine vinegar
⅓ c. olive oil
½ c. onions, minced
¼ c. parsley, minced
1 large garlic clove, minced

The deep green of parsley provides a rich contrast for tomatoes in color and flavor.

1 tsp. oregano
1 tsp. pepper
Cayenne to taste
Salt to taste

Put red wine vinegar in a small bowl and beat in olive oil in a stream. Stir in onion, parsley, garlic, oregano, pepper, cayenne, and salt. Let the mixture stand at room temperature for 2 hours, covered. Serve the sauce with broiled meats.

Makes about 1 cup.

Ancient Greeks placed wreaths of parsley on graves and sprinkled the leaves on the deceased. To say of someone that they were "ready for the parsley" was like saying they had one foot in the grave.

Rose

Rosa gallica, R. eglanteria, R. damascena, R. canina

The rose has inspired more poetry than any other blossom, but all the verse extols only its fragrance and beauty. No one has yet penned an ode to the manifold delights of rose petal preserves on hot scones. The poets of old knew well that the rose was fit for a king's lunch, since the use of roses in cooking was mentioned by Apicius, a Roman poet, gourmet, and philos-

ROSA DAMASCENA

© Derek Fell

opher, and Gerard's *Herbal* written in 1597, discusses its "fine and delectable taste" in sauces, cakes, and other dishes.

Hybrid roses are larger and better kept in florists' arrangements, as both their fragrance and flavor have been lost in the breeding. The herb gardener will want the old fashioned June-blooming roses, the kind that have grown wild along old stone walls on country roads. If the roses are not picked, most of these will "bloom" again in the fall with a crop of scarlet rose hips, full of vitamin C and tangy flavor.

Pick rosebuds to dry while they are still tightly closed, and spread them on screens in a shady, airy place. For petals, pick when the rose is just fully opened, but before blossoms begin to shatter. Hips can be snipped off as soon as they turn red.

Use fragrant rose petals in fruit compotes or sprinkle them in the bottom of a pan before pouring in white cake batter. Spread a layer of them in a cherry pie before adding the top crust. Rose sugar for tea and baking is easy to make by layering white sugar and rose petals in a jar and leaving it sealed for a few weeks. The moisture of the petals may make the sugar lumpy, in which case it can be broken up in a blender.

Floral Water

Next to lavender, the rose is the most popular herb for toiletries. Along with its fragrance, it is soothing, softening, and gently cleansing.

To make floral water to use for scent, steep one cup

© Nancy Hill

Roses respond well to growing in the espalier technique, framed against a wall. This is a favorite method in France, especially in towns where houses sit close to the street, leaving little room for shrubs.

© Jeanetta Ho

Rose hip tea is rich in vitamin C, and was drunk by the British during World War II when their supply of citrus fruit was severely limited.

of fresh rose petals in one quarter cup of ethyl alcohol for a week. Strain and store in a dark place. Rose petals in a facial sauna not only smell divine but are softening to the skin.

Rose Hip Tea

Pick rose hips when they are orange or red, and string on sturdy thread with a needle. Hang these in an airy, dry place (over or near a woodstove is a good location,

if you have one) until the hips are crisp and dry, then store in a tightly closed jar.

To make tea, crush the rose hips by whirring them in a blender. For each cup of water, use 1 teaspoon of rose hips and bring them to a full, rolling boil. Remove from the heat, cover, and let steep 15 minutes. Strain into a warmed teapot for serving hot or into a jar for chilling. Rose hip tea is tart and usually sweetened with honey. When serving iced, a sprig of lemon balm adds a refreshing fragrance. If using fresh rose hips, double the amount.

Rose Petal Preserves

4 c. rose petals
4 c. white sugar
2 c. water
Half a lemon, juiced
Lemon rind, left whole
½ tsp. cream of tartar

Combine petals and sugar and toss to distribute. Set aside for 4 to 12 hours, tossing with a fork from time to time. In a large pot bring the water to a boil and add the lemon juice, the whole lemon rind, and cream of tartar. Stir until sugar melts. Simmer over very low heat until it reaches 220°F. When it gets to 220°F, cover the pot for 10 minutes to dissolve the crystals around the edges. Remove the lemon rind. Pour into sterilized jars and seal.

Makes 4 small jars.

Crystalized Rose Petals

Candied rosebuds or petals are a delicious confection and perfect for decorating things like cakes, cream-topped pies, and parfaits. They are also delicious in iced tea if you like it sweetened. You can use the big petals from hybrid roses for this, too, but their flavor won't be quite as good or last as long.

Beat an egg white until it is no longer sticky—it does not need to be stiff, and should be a little runny. Dip petals one at a time into egg white, then in superfine sugar, coating all surfaces. Place on sheets of foil and dry in the sun (in a place sheltered from the wind) or in a 200°F oven until crisp (only a few minutes—check frequently). Store in a tightly sealed container, in layers separated by wax paper.

Rose Ice Cream

2 c. rose petals
1 c. sugar
4 c. whipping cream
¼ tsp. salt
2 to 3 drops red food coloring

Mix rose petals and sugar and let stand 4 to 12 hours. Combine with cream, salt, and food coloring and pour into an ice cream freezer and freeze as any other ice cream.

This is a light flavored, creamy, not-too-sweet ice cream that you can serve with rose preserves, with or without crushed raspberries.

Makes 1 quart of ice cream.

I know a bank whereon wild
thyme blows,
Where oxlips and the nodding
violet grows
Quite over-canopied with
luscious woodbine,
With sweet musk-roses, and
with elegantine ....

Shakespeare,
from ***Midsummer Night's Dream***

Rosemary

Rosmarinus officinalis

Rosemary is known as the herb of remembrance, and symbolizes constancy; perhaps this is because its fragrance is so long-lived, lasting for years after the leaves have dried. In cooking it is best known as a flavoring for lamb.

Rosemary is the despair of northern gardeners and those in arid climates, since it needs a humid atmosphere and will not winter well where the ground freezes deeply. It must be brought indoors in the winter in these areas and even then it often cannot survive the dry, indoor air. Mist potted plants *at least* once a week, and be careful that the soil never dries out around the roots. The prostrate, or trailing, varieties seem to live through winter more easily and will often reward their gardeners with a cascade of tiny blue blossoms in late winter. These prostrate plants adapt well to bonsai, while upright varieties can be trained as topiaries.

Rosemary roots easily from stem cuttings, but is very slow to develop from seed. In the garden it will survive drought best if it is watered from above since its leaves, as well as its roots, require moisture.

As a cosmetic herb, rosemary is the brunette's friend, adding glowing highlights to brown hair. Steep

There's Rosemary, that's for remembrance; pray you love, remember.

Shakespeare,
from *Hamlet*

PROSTRATE ROSEMARY

© Rogers Assoc.

its leaves in boiling water, cool, and add one table-spoon of cider vinegar to a cup of the tea. Use as a final hair rinse. A sprig of fresh rosemary in the bathwater is good for oily skin.

Rosemary Bonsai

Use older plants with woody stems for bonsai, since the object is to make the plant look like an ancient gnarled tree. Remove it from its pot and remove enough soil to expose the roots. Cut off the ends of all the larger roots, but handle gently to avoid damaging the tiny hair roots.

Examine your plant with a critical eye to find its best profile. The back of the plant should be slightly fuller than the front, and it should have a triangular shape. Mark a branch in some way to identify the front. Clip out some of the inner branches of the tree, but leave the upper branch that forms the tip of your triangle. Clip any branches that are taller than that one. Remove any branches that grow straight up. Think of your tree as much larger and growing on the side of a mountain, and remove those branches that look out of place. All this requires a great deal of nerve, since it seems almost ungrateful to chop at an herb plant like this!

Try moving branches to better positions, pulling branches down to lie horizontally and wire them in place with bonsai or florists' wire. Leave the wires until the branches will stay in this position without any help.

Even a fairly young rosemary plant can take on the shape of a bonsai.

Plant in a shallow pot, setting the trunk one-third of the way from edge to edge, not in the center.

Water sparingly, allowing the plant to drain well. Fertilize with half-strength houseplant food about three times a year. Trim it to maintain its shape. Repot only when growth requires it or if the soil becomes exhausted and grainy—usually every three to five years.

Rosemary Hedge

Mark out a two-foot-wide (eighty-four centimeters-wide) space and work the soil well to loosen and remove stones. Dig in rich humus so that the soil will hold moisture evenly. Mark two rows twelve inches (forty-two centimeters) apart and six inches (twenty-one centimeters) from the edges of the bed, the length of the bed. Plant well-established rosemary along these rows twelve inches (forty-two centimeters) apart and staggered. Keep well watered until plants are well established, watering from above with a fine spray during dry spells. Given a favorable climate, these hedges will grow to lush thickness and considerable height. In the castle gardens of Marvao, Portugal, such a hedge is over five feet (two meters) tall and several feet thick. Pruning will encourage branching, which fills in the center and keeps the hedge bushy.

Lamb With Orange

Follow the same recipe as for Grilled Lamb (see Oregano and Marjoram, page 103), but substitute orange juice for the wine and leave out the oregano, substituting 4 to 5 sprigs of fresh rosemary in its place. Alternate the lamb on the skewers with orange quarters, and cook as directed.

In Europe, rosemary is a traditional Christmastime potted plant, much as poinsettias are in North America. Not only is it a pinelike fragrant evergreen, but it is associated with the Virgin Mary. Legend holds that during the flight of the Holy Family, Mary stopped to wash out some of the Christ child's clothes and spread them on rosemary bushes to dry in the sun. When she did this, the bushes sprang into bloom with pale blue flowers.

Herb-Smoked Chicken

6 chicken breasts, skin intact
2 cloves garlic
3 tbsp. olive oil
2 tbsp. fresh rosemary, chopped
15 woody sprigs fresh rosemary

Rub the chicken with crushed garlic, then olive oil. Sprinkle with rosemary and let stand 1 hour. Rub the grill surface with oil. Preheat the grill. Soak the rosemary sprigs in water for at least 30 minutes. When the fire is ready, place the chicken on the grill and sear for 5 minutes, then turn and sear on the other side. Place the rosemary branches around the chicken. Cover the grill and cook 20 minutes, turning at least once. After 20 minutes, turn the chicken again. If you have a gas grill, turn off and leave covered and undisturbed for 25 minutes. For charcoal grills, douse a little water on the coals to cool them, then close the grill and open the vents. Leave undisturbed for 25 minutes. Serve with a fresh rosemary garnish.

Serves 6.

© Steven Mark Needham/Envision

Although rosemary is usually thought of as the perfect complement to lamb, it has an affinity for chicken as well.

SAGE

Sage
Salvia officinalis

Sage is one of the easiest herbs to grow from seed; it is winter hardy even in the more severe zones and is an attractive plant with a good shape. It can be air-dried by hanging and keeps its flavor well when dry.

The oval, slightly pebbly surface leaves are a dusty gray-green, and there are varieties in purple, yellow-green bicolor, and a striking tricolor sage with variations of white, green, and pink.

Pineapple sage, while in the same family, is entirely different from other culinary sages, with pointed leaves and a distinct pineapple flavor. It is a very

There are several different varieties of sage, each flavorful, and in different or mixed colors that add variety to a garden.

tender annual, but grows so profusely and quickly in a season that a single plant will provide abundant leaves to flavor teas, punches, and fruit cups. It loses its flavor when dried and loses its leaves when brought indoors, so this variety is one to enjoy straight from the garden. It is both beautiful and fragrant when used as foliage in summer bouquets, and propagates so quickly that you may find it has taken root in a vase of flowers. Use it in fruit cups or as a delicious fruity tea.

Unlike most savory herbs, sage does not blend well with other herbs. Most dishes that use sage use it alone. Its most common uses are in farm sausage and poultry stuffings, but it is also used to flavor scrapple, corn bread, and veal dishes.

Sage Onion Tart

3 medium onions, sliced
3 tbsp. butter
1 9-inch pastry crust, partially baked
3 sage leaves, minced
4 eggs
1 c. light cream

Sauté onions in butter and spread them over the bottom of a quiche pan lined with partially baked crust. Sprinkle with sage leaves. Mix eggs with light cream and pour over onions. Bake 30 minutes at 375°F or until firm and lightly browned. Serve hot or cold.

Serves 6.

Sage Onion Tart is delicious eaten hot or cold.

Saltimbocca

12 small veal scallops
12 slices Parma ham
12 leaves fresh sage
4 tbsp. butter
Salt and pepper
½ c. dry white wine

Place the veal scallops between layers of wax paper and flatten by hitting them with the broad side of a cleaver or rolling pin. Put a piece of ham and a sage leaf on each scallop and secure with a toothpick, but do not roll. Melt the butter in a large saucepan, and add the veal. Brown on both sides over a high flame for a few minutes. Salt and pepper to taste, and moisten with the wine. Cooking time should be around 5 minutes. Serve hot with the pan juices poured over the top.

Makes 12 veal scallops.

Sage Leaf Appetizer

In Italy, deep-fried sage leaves are served after dinner to aid digestion, but they make an excellent appetizer as well. Dip tender, fresh sage leaves in milk, drain excess, and dip in flour. Fry in oil at least an inch (3.5 centimeters) deep, heated to 360°F. The leaves cook quickly, so watch them carefully and remove when they are golden. Drain on paper towels and serve immediately.

This herb is so associated with wisdom and long life that we call someone old and wise a sage. Several different cultures have proverbs suggesting that it brings immortality to those who grow it.

Sage, while not as versatile as some herbs, is frequently used with poultry and veal.

SALAD BURNET

© Frances Stein

Salad Burnet

Poterium sanguisorba

One of the least known herbs, salad burnet is another reward of the garden—few people who don't grow herbs have ever tasted its cool, cucumber flavor. Delicious in salads, it is a boon to those who have trouble digesting fresh cucumbers. In a winter salad, when the only cucumbers are wax coated and tasteless, burnet vinegar brings their taste to a bowl of lettuce. In a garden, they grow in attractive mounds of finely cut leaves that can be harvested from early spring until snow covers the plants. They are very hardy, and the leaves do not lose their flavor after the plant blooms and forms seed heads. You can let them mature and scatter to form volunteer plants or you can pick mature heads and bury them where you want new plants to grow.

Although their main use is in salads, they are also floated in aperitif wines and can replace the sliver of cucumber peel in a Pimm's cup.

Thomas Jefferson was a great proponent of salad burnet, which he used for livestock forage. Its use as a medicine, especially for blood-related complaints, dates to Roman times.

Burnet Vinegar

Half fill a canning jar with fresh-picked burnet leaves, and add red wine vinegar until the jar is full. Allow to steep for two to three weeks before using. The leaves do not turn pale, as do those of most herbs when steeped in vinegar, so they may be rinsed off and chopped into salads when the plant is no longer available. But the vinegar alone will provide cucumber flavor to a salad.

The even mead that erst brought
     forth
**The freckled Cowslip, Burnet,
     and Sweet Clover.**

          Shakespeare,
          from *Henry V*

One of the most useful herb vinegars is made with salad burnet, which lends its fresh cucumber flavor to winter salads.

Parsley is a good herb to pair with the fresh, delicate flavor of salad burnet.

Herbed Yogurt Cheese Balls

1 c. plain yogurt
2½ c. olive oil
*3 to 6 sprigs fresh herbs—salad burnet, chive,
     parsley*

Stir the yogurt until smooth, and place in the center of a large piece of cheesecloth that is 2 to 3 layers thick. Tie into a bundle. Tie the bundle onto the handle of a wooden spoon and suspend over a deep pan, making sure the cheesecloth does not touch the bottom of the pan. Let drain overnight. Unwrap and shape into balls with your fingers; it should make about 15 small balls. Pour the olive oil into a jar, add the cheese balls, and tuck the herbs down the edges. Cover and let sit at least 2 days before eating. Serve with crackers.

Tarragon

Artemisia dracunculus

The darling of French chefs, tarragon has a distinguished history in the kitchen. Its delicate flavor enhances chicken, veal, and seafood. White wine vinegar in which tarragon leaves have been steeped is an essential ingredient of béarnaise sauce. Popular throughout Europe, it has not always been common in the New World, although Thomas Jefferson treasured the plants in his garden.

Tarragon does not grow from seed. If you are offered seed for this plant, as some seed houses do, you can be sure that it is for the weedy, tasteless relative, Russian tarragon, which will soon take over your garden and give no more taste to your dinner than an equal amount of grass clippings. The culinary tarragon does not set seed and is propagated entirely from root or stem cuttings. Although there have been reports from time to time of true French tarragon setting seed or growing from seed, none has been authenticated by any botanical authority, and it is likely that on these occasions it was really an unusually flavorful plant of Russian tarragon, which does sometimes happen. Until one is authenticated, it is safe to assume that culinary tarragon needs to be propagated from cuttings or divisions of a known plant.

The roots of tarragon tend to grow inward, twisting tighter and tighter, so it is usually best to dig it up every third spring and divide the root to reset it. This ensures more vigorous plants as well as increasing their numbers. Although tarragon will tolerate light shade, it does best in full sun, in well-drained soil.

The leaves may be used fresh anytime, and the plant can be cut twice during the season for drying, the final cutting to remove nearly all of the growing stems before winter. Leave the bottom branches in the garden to identify where it will come up during the next season. In areas where the temperature dips well be-

TARRAGON

© Rogers Assoc.

low freezing without a ground covering of snow, it is best to provide tarragon with a light covering of winter mulch (salt hay, loose straw, or pine boughs all work well) to protect its roots from alternate freezing and thawing.

Although tarragon retains its flavor fairly well if dried very quickly, there is no substitute for fresh tarragon, which has many times the flavor of dried. Also, several favorite uses of the herb are best done with entire sprigs. For example, the meat of a roast chicken will be subtly permeated with flavor if sprigs of the fresh herb are placed between the skin and the breast meat. Likewise, a sprig of tarragon laid in the cavity of a fish while it is being cooked helps to moderate the "fishy" flavor.

© Rogers Assoc.

Proving that herb gardening is not solely a country pastime, Chef Kevin Gownley of the Sazerec Restaurant in the Hotel Fairmont, New Orleans, Louisiana, harvests flavorings for dinner in his lush herb garden on the hotel's roof.

Veal Medallions with Wild Mushrooms and Tarragon Dijon Butter Sauce

This recipe was created by Kevin Gownley, chef of the Sazerac Restaurant in the Fairmont Hotel, New Orleans. The Fairmont maintains a full herb garden on its roof and chef Gownley begins his day there, selecting the herbs that will mark that day's specialties.

2 sticks (½ c.) plus 1 tbsp. butter, kept cold, and
all but 2 tbsp. diced into small chunks

4 shallots, peeled and chopped
2 sprigs fresh tarragon with stems, chopped
1 pt. dry white wine
1 c. heavy cream
1 tbsp. fresh tarragon leaves, chopped
3 to 4 tbsp. Dijon mustard
Salt and white pepper to taste
½ lb. mixed wild mushrooms (shiitake, morels, etc.)
2 tbsp. vegetable oil
8 3-oz. veal medallions (2 per person)

Melt 1 tablespoon of butter in a skillet; sauté half of the shallots and the chopped tarragon with stems. Pour in the white wine and reduce until it is almost evaporated. Pour in the cream and reduce it by half. Add all the diced butter, whipping it, to emulsify the sauce. When the butter is half melted, remove the sauce from the heat and continue whipping it until the butter is fully incorporated. Strain the sauce through a mesh sieve. Add the chopped tarragon leaves and mustard. Season with salt and white pepper to taste. Keep the sauce warm.

Remove the mushroom stems and save them for other uses. Cut the caps into fine, matchstick shapes. Melt the remaining tablespoon of butter in another sauté pan and sauté the remaining shallots until they are transluscent, about 30 seconds. Add the julienned mushroom caps and sauté 2 minutes. Season with salt

Veal Medallions Tarragon makes an elegant entree served with baby courgettes and crookneck squash steamed fresh from the vegetable garden.

and pepper. Set aside in a warm area, but not over heat.

Put the oil in a saucepan and heat until it begins to smoke. Season the medallions with salt and white pepper and sauté them quickly over high heat until they are medium rare, about 1 minute per side. Remove them from the pan and drain them on paper towels.

On four ovenproof dinner plates, mound mushrooms in the center and top each mound with two medallions, slightly overlapping. Place the plates in an oven preheated to 500°F for 30 to 60 seconds until they are hot. Garnish with vegetables, and spoon the warm sauce over the medallions and mushrooms. Serve immediately.

Makes 4 servings.

Fresh Scampi Bisque Grinkle Park

The following recipe comes from the Grinkle Park Hotel, situated in the manor house of a shooting estate on the coast of North Yorkshire, near Easington. The chef uses the bounty of the sea and the wild game of the moors as well as the abundance of locally grown herbs.

> *2 oz. butter*
> *2 lbs. fresh scampi*
> *1 onion, chopped*
> *1½ pt. good fish stock*
> *¼ pt. dry white wine*

A sprig of parsley or tarragon can be used to garnish this scampi bisque, a specialty of Grinkle Park, near Whitby, England.

© Burke/Triolo

Pinch fresh tarragon
½ pt. heavy cream
Corn flour to thicken
Beurre manie (2 oz. softened butter mixed with
  2 oz. flour)

In a large, thick-bottomed saucepan melt the butter and sauté the onion and scampi slightly, taking care not to let them color. Add the white wine, fish stock, and tarragon. Bring to a boil, reduce heat, and simmer for 20 minutes. Thicken with the *beurre manie* and cook for 10 minutes. Put into a blender for a few seconds and strain through a fine wire sieve. Put into a fresh saucepan and heat. If the sauce is too thin correct by mixing in corn flour and water. Correct seasoning. Finish with cream just before serving.

Makes 4 servings.

Coddled Eggs

Eggs
Fresh black pepper
Fresh tarragon leaves
1 tbsp. butter
1 tsp. cream

Butter the inside of each egg coddler generously, and lightly salt the inside. Break an egg into each coddler. Add a grinding of fresh black pepper, a few leaves of fresh tarragon, a dab of butter, and the cream. Close

the coddler and, when all coddlers are prepared, submerge them in boiling water. Continue to boil—about 4 to 5 minutes for a soft boiled egg. The blessing of coddlers is that you can remove a lid and check to see if it is cooked just the way you like it.

Tartar Sauce

1 egg
1 c. mayonnaise, homemade is preferable but a
  good prepared one is fine
1 tbsp. onion, minced
½ small dill pickle
1 tbsp. capers
⅛ c. fresh, stemless parsley leaves
1 tbsp. fresh tarragon leaves
1 tbsp. fresh lemon juice
¼ tsp. hot red pepper sauce
Salt and pepper to taste

Put the egg in a small pan and cover it with water. Put the pan onto a hot burner and bring it to a boil. Remove it from the heat and set it aside for 12 minutes. Cool and peel the egg and mince it. Mix the egg into the mayonnaise. Mince the onion, pickle, capers, parsley, and tarragon and mix into the mayonnaise. Add 1 tablespoon of lemon juice and the hot red pepper sauce to the mixture and stir together. Season with salt and pepper to taste.

Makes approximately ½ cup of tartar sauce.

Tarragon Mayonnaise Sauce, Buena Vista Palace

This is a favorite recipe of the Buena Vista Palace Hotel at Lake Buena Vista in Orlando, Florida, where they serve it with their lobster salad. It is equally good on chilled shrimp, crabmeat, or cold chicken.

> *4 eggs*
> *1 tbsp. mustard*
> *2 c. salad oil*
> *½ oz. fresh tarragon, chopped*
> *Salt and pepper to taste*
> *Juice of ½ lemon*

THYME

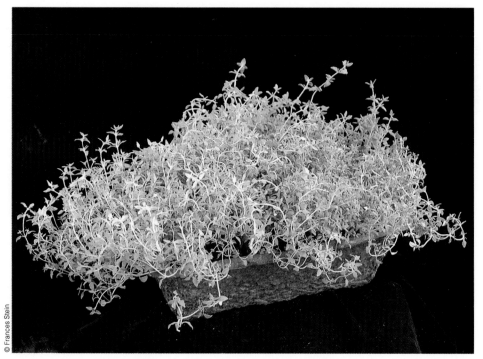

© Frances Stein

Whip the eggs and the mustard together. Continue to beat the eggs while slowly adding the oil and tarragon. Add salt and pepper to taste, then whip and slowly add the lemon juice.

Makes approximately 1 pint of sauce.

Thyme

Thymus vulgaris; Lemon Thyme: *Thymus citriodorus*

One of the mainstays of cooking, thyme is the wallflower of the herb shelf, blending inconspicuously into the flavors of soups, stews, sauces, marinades, and meat dishes without attracting attention to itself. It is just as modest in the herb garden, with low growth and inconspicuous blooms. In either place it is a joy to encounter.

Thyme may be started from seed, but is more quickly established from plants propagated by stem layering (see page 31). Its flavor is strongest just before it blooms, but even afterward the fragrant leaves have plenty of flavor. Its tiny blossoms are a favorite of bees, and the honey is excellent wherever wild thyme grows. The plants do exceptionally well in seashore areas where the constant humidity keeps them lush and green.

Thyme makes a handsome low "hedge" around herb beds and is especially attractive against brick walks.

In a few years a single thyme plant will spread to a tidy clump by self-layering, but very often the center, with the woody stems, will begin to die back leaving a ring instead of a mound. When this begins to happen, carefully cut the newly rooted stems from the original plant so that there are no connecting stems between it and the new plants. Dig out the original plant cautiously, being careful not to disturb the new plants. Fill the hole with fresh soil. Transplant some of the outer, newly rooted plants to the area. By the next year the clump will be healthy and solid again.

In the fall, harvest thyme by cutting it back to the woody growth, leaving some foliage near the base. Common thyme withstands very cold winters, even without snow, but the more delicate lemon thyme may need mulching and may even die from the cold.

After the thyme has dried and you have stripped all of the leaves from the woody stems, save the stems and lay them over the coals when you are grilling chicken or meat. For a smoked herb flavor, soak the stems in warm water for a half hour before using.

Thyme has a special affinity for game and shellfish and no New England chowder would taste right without it. It is easy to use in fresh sprigs, since the leaves stay on the stem during cooking and the whole sprig can easily be removed before serving.

A Living Wreath of Thyme

Fill a double-wire wreath frame (these can be purchased at any florist shop) with sphagnum moss, making sure that it is firm, and soak overnight in water. Place on a plate with a slight rim or in a shallow bowl. Insert rooted thyme into the sphagnum at three-inch (eleven-centimeter) intervals. For a more beautiful wreath, alternate common thyme with lemon, silver, or golden varieties. Other herbs, such as rosemary, may be added for accent. Keep evenly moist by pouring water into the center of the dish, and add a few drops of fertilizer with each watering.

Begin this wreath when you do your final garden pruning and shaping in October and it will be ready by December. To add candles, simply set them in small holders in the center of the wreath and pull the herb sprigs around them. If you don't have plants that are already rooted, use soft green cuttings and dip them in rooting hormone before inserting into the frame. A

To the ancient Greeks, thyme symbolized courage. In the Middle Ages, ladies stitched a sprig of thyme into handkerchiefs they gave to knights going into battle. It came to the New World with the earliest settlers and has naturalized in some areas, including the north shore of Prince Edward Island, in Canada, where roadsides are purple with its bloom in midsummer.

wreath done this way will take longer to grow lush and full. When any stem becomes straggly, simply weave it back in to cover a bare spot. Misting every week will keep it fresh all winter.

Venison Conserve

2 qts. stemmed fox grapes or Concord grapes
1 lemon, ground or finely chopped
½ c. raisins
6 c. sugar
1 cinnamon stick
2 sprigs fresh thyme

Pop skins from the grapes and cook the pulp over low heat until soft, adding only enough water to prevent sticking. Meanwhile, grind the skins. Press the pulp through a food mill to remove the seeds, and combine with the skins in a heavy pot. Add the remaining ingredients and slowly bring to a boil, stirring often. Reduce heat and simmer until thick, about 1 hour, stirring frequently to prevent sticking. Remove the thyme and the cinnamon stick and pour into sterile jars. Seal and process in boiling water for 10 minutes. Serve with venison or other game.

Makes 6 jars of conserve.

Thyme Marinade for Venison

1 bunch fresh thyme
1 bottle dry red wine

Lay the herbs on the bottom of a flat container and place venison medallions on them. Pour wine over the meat, cover, and let marinate in the refrigerator for 3 days, turning the meat at least once daily. This recipe is at its most splendid when done with loin medallions, which are then very lightly sautéed in butter and served immediately.

Makes 3 cups of marinade.

Fresh thyme is a staple of the French soup pot and is sold in large bundles in Paris markets such as this one at Montparnasse.

© Rogers Assoc.

Thyme Salad Dressing

½ c. olive oil
3 tbsp. balsamic vinegar
Fresh ground pepper to taste
4 sprigs fresh thyme
1 clove garlic, peeled

Combine the ingredients in a jar and shake well. Let stand at least overnight before using on fresh salads. Be sure that the garlic and the thyme do not fall out into the salad.

Makes ½ cup of dressing.

Cabernet Butter Sauce for Grouper

This savory sauce is served at the Buena Vista Palace Hotel at Lake Buena Vista, Orlando, Florida.

1 carrot, finely chopped
1 onion, finely chopped
1 stalk celery, finely chopped
1 clove garlic, finely chopped
1 oz. smoked ham, finely chopped
3 tbsp. butter
2 sprigs fresh thyme
1 fresh bay leaf
Pinch of cracked black peppercorns
¼ bottle Cabernet
4 c. heavy cream

Sauté the carrot, onion, celery, garlic, and ham in butter until well-coated. Add herbs and pepper and cook, covered, over lowest heat until the onions are transparent. Stir in the wine and simmer until reduced by half. Add cream and simmer very gently to reduce and thicken. Strain the sauce and serve over grouper or other fish.

Maryland Crab Soup, Kent Manor Inn

This recipe is a specialty of the Kent Manor Inn whose gracious dining room overlooks the Chesapeake Bay on Kent Island, near Annapolis, Maryland.

3 qts. water
2 lbs. beef bones
2 16 oz. cans of tomatoes, diced, with juice
1 large onion, finely chopped
3 stalks celery with tops, finely chopped
2 large carrots, finely chopped
4 large ears Silver Queen corn, cut from cob
1½ c. fresh snipped green beans, coarsely chopped
1 c. fresh baby lima beans
½ c. fresh green peas (young)
1 small head cabbage, coarsely chopped
3 medium potatoes, peeled and diced
½ c. old bay seasoning
2 tbsp. fresh thyme
2 tbsp. salt
1 tsp. black pepper
½ lb. fresh backfin crabmeat
6 blue crabs, cleaned, steamed, and quartered

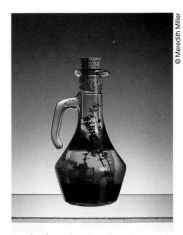

Look for elegant bottles and cruets as gift containers for your own herb salad dressings.

I know a bank where the wild Thyme grows.

Shakespeare,
from *Midsummer Night's Dream*

In a large soup stockpot, add water, beef bones, tomatoes, onions, celery, and carrots. Bring to a boil, reduce heat, and simmer for 40 minutes. Add the other fresh vegetables and spices and continue to simmer for 1 hour and 20 minutes, until they are tender. Remove the bones and add the crabmeat. The soup may have reduced, and if needed add more water to achieve the desired consistency. Add the quartered blue crabs to the tureen as garnish.

Makes about 28 bowls of soup.

To throw a perfume on the violet
Is wasteful and ridiculous excess.

Shakespeare,
from *King John*

BLUE VIOLETS

© John A. Lynch/Photo/Nats

Violet

Viola odorata

Nothing symbolizes spring quite like bunches of sweet purple violets. Flower sellers, from the streets of London to the Indian markets of the Andes in Ecuador, offer nosegays of these. In France, candied violets are passed around at the end of a meal, and the leaves are eaten as a tasty spring tonic salad.

In the garden, they are one of the first flowers of spring, blooming with the tulips. They are perennial, growing from small root clumps in clusters of heart-shaped leaves. They form new clumps easily, and may

© Rogers Assoc.

WHITE VIOLETS

be removed in late summer or moved to another spot. Violets are at their loveliest growing between rocks in a stone wall. They will grow well in shade or sun.

The delicate flavor and fragrance of violet blossoms leads to their use as a decoration for cakes and petit fours. The flowers are also used to garnish chilled cream soups and scoops of sherbet. For a special touch, float a violet blossom in a glass of chilled white wine.

Candied, the blossoms will keep for a few weeks if sealed and stored in a cool place. The leaves are a soothing addition to a warm bath, and violet-leaf tea is good for washing dry or sensitive skin.

Violet Jam

1 pkg. powdered pectin
2½ c. water
½ c. lemon juice
3 c. sugar
1 c. violet blossoms, tightly packed

Combine the pectin, water, and lemon juice and bring to a boil; add the sugar all at once, stir, and boil for 3 minutes. Stir in the violets and remove from the heat immediately. Pour into hot sterilized jars and seal. Process 5 minutes in boiling water.

In England, this jam is taken as a vitamin supplement, but it is too tasty and beautiful to treat as medicine. Try putting a "dose" of it on hot scones.

Makes 2 to 3 jars of jam.

Spring Salad

Toss a handful each of violets, spinach, and tiny dandelion leaves with a small head of tender spring lettuce. Mix with thyme dressing (see page 137) and sprinkle with chopped chives and violet flowers.

Crystalized Violets

Boil 1 cup of water with 1 pound of sugar to make a heavy syrup, and continue boiling until the syrup reaches 240°F. Drop flowers into the syrup a few at a time and let sit 1 minute. Remove carefully with a fork and lay face down on aluminum foil to dry. Spread the petals carefully, sliding wooden skewers or toothpicks under them to smooth them. When all violets are dipped, set the foil in a preheated 250°F oven with the door slightly ajar until the flowers are dry. Turn them over when they have dried enough to keep their shape.

Brush with egg white and sprinkle with superfine sugar as for mint leaves (see page 109). They can be stored only a few days.

© Steven Mark Needham/Envision

Violets were the symbol of ancient Athens, and were thought to spring up wherever Orpheus stepped. Long associated with lovers, the violet was a token of love between Napoleon and Josephine and later became his emblem. Today, they are the favorite flower for filling May baskets. In the Victorian language of flowers, they represented modesty and humility.

Sources

Seeds, Plants, and Garden Accessories

Alberta Nurseries and Seed, Ltd.
P.O. Box 20
Bowden, Alberta, T0M OK0 Canada

Gardener's Collection
Deline Lake, P.O. Box 243
Sydenham, Ontario, K0H 2T0 Canada
(Stoneware garden markers)

Jackson and Perkins Co.
P.O. Box 1028
Medford, OR 97501
(Roses)

Nichols Garden Nursery
1190 North Pacific Highway
Albany, OR 97321

Owens Farms
Curve Nankipoo Road
Route 3, Box 158A
Ripley, TN 38063

Shepherd's Garden Seeds
30 Irene Street
Torrington, CT 06790

Taylor's Herb Gardens
1535 Lone Oak Road
Vista, CA 92084

Andre Viette Farm and Nursery
Route 1, Box 16
Fishersville, VA 22939

Supplies and Materials

Bob Clark
901 Sheridan Drive
Lancaster, OH 43130
(Ceramic potpourri jars)

Herbitage Farm
Old Homestead Highway
Richmond, NH 03470
(Herb craft kits and books)

Rosemary House
120 South Market Street
Mechanicsburg, PA 17055
(Gathering baskets, herb supplies, and gifts)

The Swinging Bridge Pottery
S.R. 2, Box 395
Criglersville, VA 22727
(Garden markers, pots, and herb jars)

Publications

The Herb Companion
306 North Washington
Loveland, CO 80537
(Magazine)

The Herbal Gazette
Rt. 1, Box 105
Checotah, OK 74426
(Newsletter)

The Joy of Herbs
P.O. Box 7617
Birmingham, AL 35253-0617
(Magazine)

New Hampshire Herb Society
P.O. Box 142
Warner, NH 03278
(Newsletter and events)

Potpourri From Herbal Acres
Pine Row Publications
Box 428
Washington Crossing, PA 18977
(Newsletter and network)

Cookbooks for Cuisines Rich in Herbs

Come With Me to the Kasbah: A Cook's Tour
*   of Morocco*
by Kitty Morse
La Caravane
P.O. Box 433
Vista, CA 92083
$24.95 plus $3.00 shipping
(Beautifully illustrated guide to a
    little-explored cuisine)

The Cuisines of Mexico
by Diana Kennedy
Harper and Row
$14.95
(The definitive work on Mexico's varied
    cooking styles)

La Varenne Practique: The Complete
*   Illustrated Cooking Course*
by Anne Willan
Crown Publishers
$60.00
(Illustrated with 2,500 full color photographs)

Lebanese Mountain Cookery
by Mary Hamady
David R. Godine Publishers
$19.95
(Fresh herbs in unusual settings)

Prima Piatti: Italian First Courses that Make
*   a Meal*
by Christopher Styler
Harper and Row
$22.95
(Some of the finest Italian herb uses)

Restaurants Mentioned in the Text

Arthur's 27
Buena Vista Palace
Buena Vista, FL 32830

Chiangmai
Route 101A
Amherst, NH 03031

Grinkle Park
Easington, Saltburn-by-the-Sea
Cleveland TS13 4UB, England

Hemingway's
Route 4
Killington, VT 05751

Kent Manor Inn
Route 8-S
Kent Island, MD 21666

Sazerac Restaurant
Hotel Fairmont
New Orleans, LA 70100

Index